WE LIKE THINGS TOO

read why

ace & tate

THE BOILING-WATER TAP
WITH FLEXIBLE PULL OUT HOSE

The Flex is Quooker's latest innovation. The world's first 100°C boiling-water tap, equipped with a flexible pull out hose for hot, cold and filtered cold water. Thanks to the boiling-water stop, the Flex cannot dispense boiling water when the hose is pulled out, making it 100% safe to use.

Interested?
Visit a dealer, go to quooker.co.uk or call 0345 833 3333 for more information.

Book, Chair, Oil Container

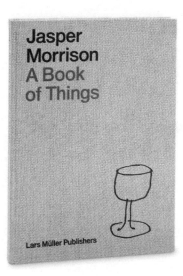

jaspermorrisonshop.com

24b Kinglsand Road
London, E2 8DA

Monday – Friday
11am – 5pm

20–23 September 2018

The largest collection of international exhibitions, designers, brands, country pavilions and galleries in one destination during the London Design Festival.

londondesignfair.co.uk

Old Truman Brewery
E1 6QR

PRE-REGISTER FOR YOUR TRADE PASS NOW

BACK IN BUSINESS THE

COMPACT DIABOLO

1990 / 2018

DESIGNER
ARNOLD MERCKX

Twentieth and Twenty-First Century Collectible Design

December 5–9, 2018/
Miami Beach, USA/
@designmiami #designmiami
designmiami.com

Design/
Miami/

Dolphin Chair/ Hans J. Wegner, 1950/ Courtesy of Galleri Feldt

4. THE LIFE OF THINGS

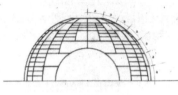

5. APPENDIX

We do not belong to that group of people who see the ball as the greatest invention of humankind. No game without a ball, and no human without a game, they say. At the age of 13, this was something that we, excuse the pun, roundly rejected. We saw the ball as the embodiment of evil — a malevolent tool that our classmates could use to pillory us. 'Dodgeball' was the appropriate name of the game with which we, after the humiliation of being the last to get picked, were slaughtered in the high school gym. Our gym teacher found it amusing to conclude our weekly torture with the same question: 'How many sides does a football have?' 'An inside and an outside,' was our mumbled reply.

Perhaps that's why we still don't watch football matches. But the ball itself fascinates us. Which other object has its own newspaper sections and television channels? It is one of the few things that is not a basic necessity of life, but still ubiquitous. It's probably not just the game that explains the worship of the ball. The perfection of the round shape and the almost impossible task of producing perfectly round balls also contribute to its adoration. 'A sphere, at all times, is equal only to itself; it is the perfect symbol of equality,' wrote architect Boullée in the 18th century. 'No body possesses, as it does, this exceptional quality: that each of its facets is equal to all the other.' This equality is also important in sports — which explains why, for every World Cup Football, there is such a manic quest for and deliberation on the design and properties of the Tango, Azteca, Etrusco, Questra, Tricolore, Teamgeist, Jabulani or Brazuca ball.

In ancient Greece the gods played football with the world. It is an image that could illustrate the everyday but simultaneously mythical attraction of the ball; a representation of the earth and the universe in which we live, but that we also like to kick against; nearby and elusive. Perhaps that's why many Dutch football clubs are named after Greek gods, such as Heracles or Ajax. And why for designers, architects, astrologers, philosophers, utopians, demolishers, athletes, science fiction writers and club owners, the ball is an item that not only rolls, but also beholds. 'With an inside and an outside', as our sports teacher would say.

Kirsten Algera
Ernst van der Hoeven
Editors

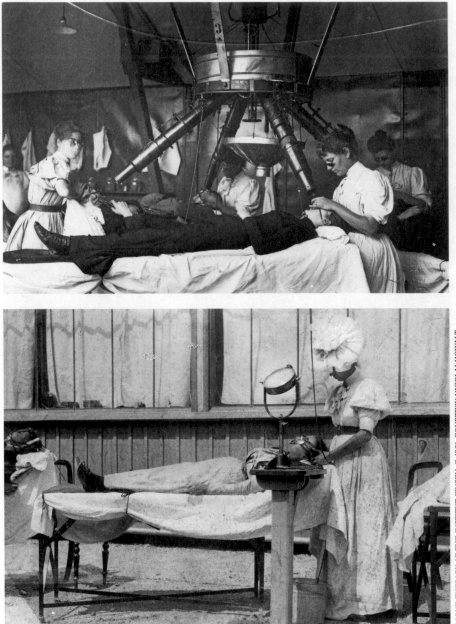

LIGHT THERAPY AT THE INSTITUT FINSEN, C. 1901. COURTESY NICOLAI HOWALT

LIGHT BREAK

Danish artist Nicolai Howalt (1970) investigates and visualizes the typical effect of solar radiation using a scientific method of 19th-century phototherapy, invented by Niels Ryberg Finsen (1860–1904). This unique method of light exposure resulted in a series of imprints of projected and filtered sunrays on photosensitive paper (C-print). Using certain filters and rock crystal lenses, Finsen proved that certain wavelengths of light can have a therapeutic effect. With the help of Finsen's original coloured filters and lenses, Howart was able to absorb selected areas of light and pass the remaining areas through Finsen's original rock-crystal lenses and contemporary coloured lenses onto photosensitive C-print paper.

Nicolai Howalt, *Wavelength N° 644, 0 nanometer*, *Wavelength N° 703, 2 nanometer*, *Wavelength N° 564, 0 nanometer*, *Wavelength N° 610, 1 nanometer* and *Wavelength N° 539, 6 nanometer* from the series *Lightbreak*, 2015

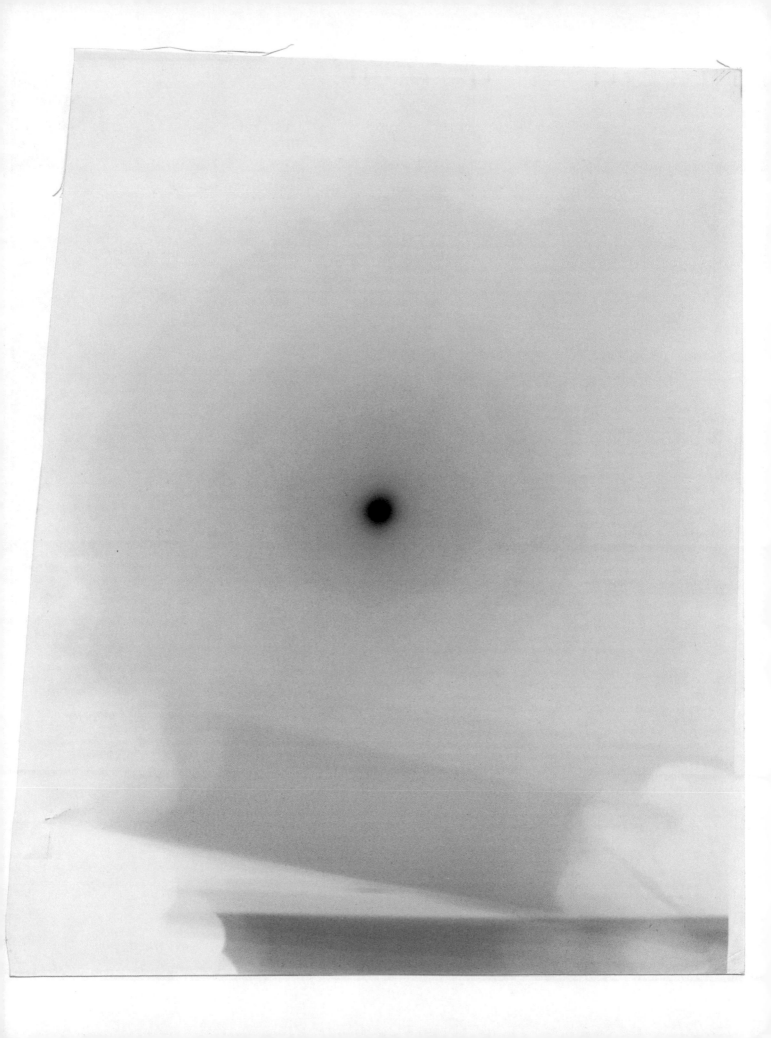

1.
TO ROLL

Ball boys and girls fetch them, typewriters hit them, Adidas sews them and biros hide them. Part 1 rounds up lots of balls that roll around our world.

Latex ball of Olmec origin, around 1600 BCE, Mexico. Photo Kenneth Garrett

THE BOUNCIEST

On the 15 June 1844, Charles Goodyear patented a chemical process for converting latex from a rubber tree into a more durable material by mixing it with sulphur and white lead and by heating this compound to a certain temperature. To honour the man and his invention, a tyre factory was named after him.

Goodyear may have invented the process of vulcanization, but he wasn't the first to produce durable rubber. Thousands of years before him, Mesoamerican civilizations knew that if you mixed latex with the juice from morning glory vines, you got a substance that is perfect for making sandals, bands

and, above all, balls. The oldest such balls date from around 1600 BCE. They vary in size from a squash ball to a beach ball and were used for ceremonial ball games played on stone-walled courts.

When Christopher Columbus returned home after his second voyage to the New World, he brought some as a gift for King Charles V. Those who witnessed the balls being sent into the air after hitting the ground couldn't believe their eyes. The elastic orb was nothing like the lifeless leather spheres filled with hair, feathers and air that they used to play early versions of tennis or football.

The incredible bounce was a result of Pre-Columbian chemistry. The Aztecs and Maya not only knew how to make rubber, but also had different recipes for different purposes. For bouncy balls they used a mixture with fifty percent juice. Sandals were made from a blend with 25 percent juice. And to acquire the strongest rubber bands, no juice was added. So more than 3,400 years before Goodyear received U.S. Patent No. 3,633 for his 'useful improvements', the Mesoamericans were successfully engineering materials to suit their needs.

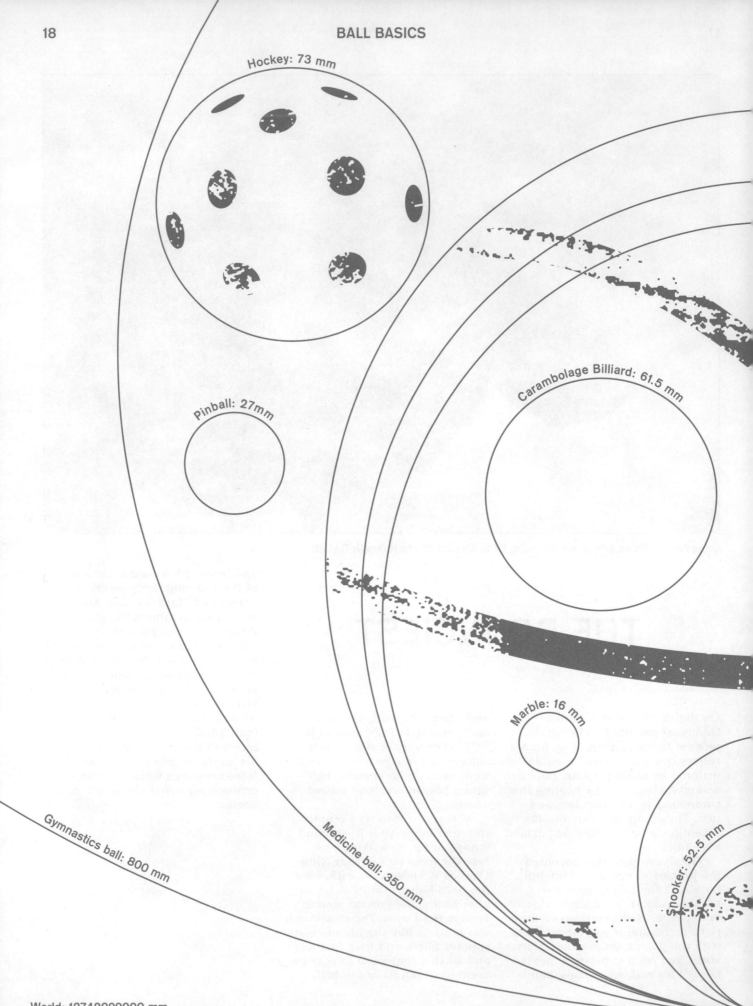

Hockey: 73 mm

Carambolage Billiard: 61.5 mm

Pinball: 27mm

Marble: 16 mm

Snooker: 52.5 mm

Gymnastics ball: 800 mm

Medicine ball: 350 mm

World: 12742000000 mm

Ballpoint: 0.5 mm

Basketball: 240 mm

Soccer: 221 mm

Beach Volleyball: 210 mm

Pool Billiard: 57 mm

Russian Billiard: 68 mm

Baseball: 75 mm

Golf: 43 mm

All values refer to the diameter. The balls are shown at full scale.

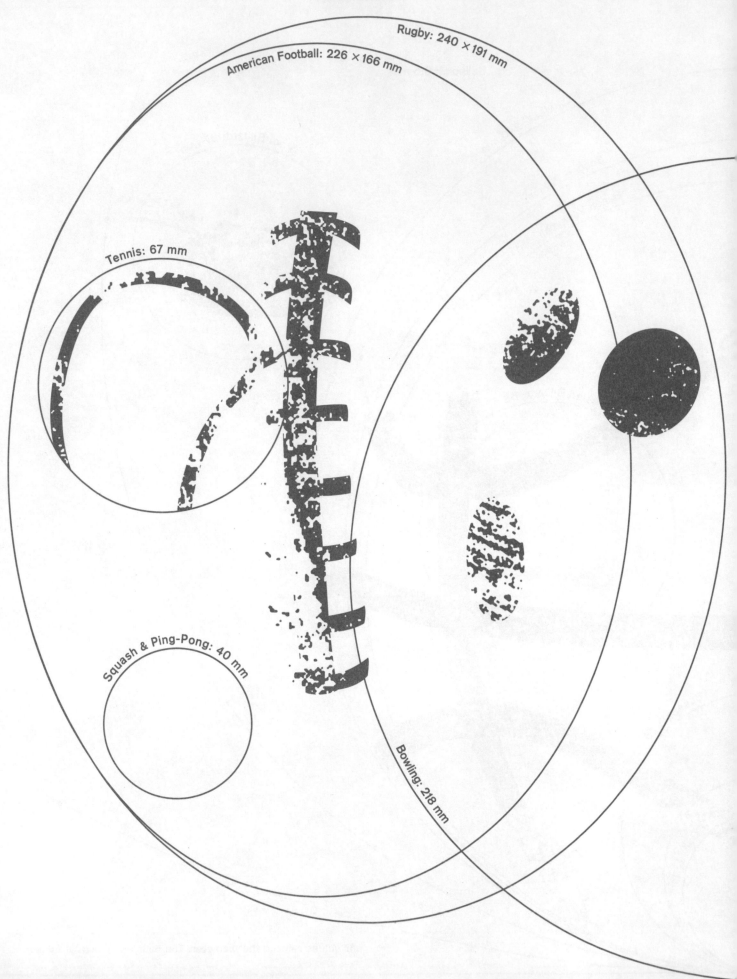

Rugby: 240 × 191 mm

American Football: 226 × 166 mm

Tennis: 67 mm

Squash & Ping-Pong: 40 mm

Bowling: 218 mm

BBGs

Top-class sport just wouldn't be the same without them, those reassuring boys and girls who scamper around the court, pitch or field of play to keep our sporting superstars supplied with balls.

Text by Eliot Haworth

Chelsea keeper William 'Fatty' Foulke, 1905

There they go. Scuttling about on the peripheries of sports fields. Gamely hunting down balls when no one else will — ball boys. Anyone who has played a game of tennis, football, or just about any other ball-based pastime at an amateur level will know how much time can be lost retrieving errant balls. Thanks to our clumsy efforts they go careering off fields of play, flying into bushes, pinging over fences, thwacking into nets. Enter the ball boy. The brave and obliging individuals who, with little desire for fame or recognition, keep athletes in fresh supply of bouncy balls and make sure our favourite sports never miss a beat.

The origin of the ball boy is murky. Fetching balls is tedious, and we often take it for granted that we use ball boys to speed up the process of playing sport; it's seemingly always been that way. They are actually an ingenious time and energy saving innovation and must have a point of origin. Balls have been used for sporting purposes almost continuously throughout human history, but whether or not ancient Greek or Mayan athletes ever thought to get someone else to gather them up is unclear. As it happens, the first widely reported use of ball boys dates only as far back as the dawn of the 20th century and the early years of professional football in England. It also happened completely accidentally.

In 1905 the newly formed Chelsea Football Club signed the goalkeeper William 'Fatty' Foulke from Sheffield United for a sum of £50. As his nickname suggests, Foulke was a large man, and at 6 foot 4 inches (193 cm) and 23 stone (146 kg) he towered over his teammates and opposition (the average height for a male at the time was just under 5 foot 6 inches or 168 cm). This was a considerable advantage in a game in which it was still legal to shove a goalkeeper over the goal line along with the ball. Foulke's size and impressive performances had already made him a celebrity by the time he joined Chelsea, and to play up to the larger-than-life image of their star signing they devised a gimmick: every time 'Fatty' walked onto the field of play at the beginning of the match, he was flanked by two small boys to make him appear even larger. The boys were then positioned behind the goal, one by each post, to maintain the optical illusion throughout the match. This also had another unexpected advantage; Foulke started getting the boys to collect the ball for him whenever it went behind his goal, helping him to save energy and to speed up play. When other teams began to pick up on this advantage they copied the trick, and as the legend goes, the ball boy was born, spawning a rich and varied universe of ball retrieving whizz-kids.

BALL BOY MASTERMINDS

It did not take long for ball boys to catch on in other sports, with Wimbledon becoming the first tennis tournament to introduce them in the 1920s, and with all grand slam tennis tournaments now using them. The modern-day tennis ball boy is without a doubt the most rigorously drilled in the world of sport. They exude a discipline and focus of mind on par with that of most athletes. Each tournament has a stringent selection process. At Wimbledon each year, 250 BBGs (Ball Boys and Girls) are selected from 1,000 applicants drawn from local schools in South West London. At the

Previous page: Serena Williams versus Maria Sharapova, Australian Open 2016

Novak Djokovic versus Rafael Nadal, Wimbledon 2018

French Open the numbers are even higher; this year a national competition ran, drawing 4,200 applicants, with only 220 selected. The Australian Open also holds a national selection process through their 'National Ballkid Programme' for children aged 12–15, while things operate a little differently in the United States where the term 'ball person' is used not so much to denote a mix of genders (which there is) but a mix of ages. (A US Open ball person is more of a job than a voluntary role and attracts teens on their summer break from college, adults looking for part-time work and tennis-mad professionals who far exceed any possible definition of a 'ball boy' but just want to be close to the action.)

The training programmes are intensive. Wimbledon BBGs train regularly from February until the tournament in July — although the majority also train independently at their respective schools from the autumn onwards — while French Open ball kids, the majority of them youth players, partake in a year-long training and selection process. At these boot camps the prospective applicants undergo written tests, fitness tests, speed tests, and hand-eye coordination tests. They develop the core ball boy skills: rolling, feeding and receiving.

Feeding and receiving are the processes by which ball boys and girls deliver new balls, and towels and drinks, to players and receive any balls back from players or from fellow ball boys. Rolling is perhaps the most important skill, as it is the primary method by which balls are circulated on court. If a ball boy cannot roll a ball quickly in a straight flat line they will not make the cut. (The exception, once again, is the US Open, where ball persons throw the ball the length of the court instead.)

They must also practice keeping perfect posture and are drilled in various set pieces such as how to walk out at the beginning of a game and the many quirks of players they might encounter (Andy Murray, for instance, always wants a towel in hands after every point, while Maria Sharapova asks to receive her balls from the same side during a game). A good pain threshold is also a bonus, as many ball boys are also on the receiving end of stray shots and serves — which might not sound too bad until you watch

Roger Federer versus Rafael Nadal, Australian Open 2012

a video of an Australian Open ball boy taking a 196 km/h serve to the crotch.

All this comes together to form a cohesive ball boy machine that, at its best, should be almost imperceptible to the spectators, keeping a steady supply of balls provided throughout a match. In most major tournaments the ball boys are continually assessed and graded each day, with cuts made at each round of the tournament. Meaning that as the strongest players progress towards the final, so do the strongest ball boys.

Compared to tennis, with its endlessly complex systems and responsibilities, football ball boys — despite being the more historic profession — have far less required of them. Their role amounts to a single basic task: throw the ball back when it goes off the pitch. Yet it would be a mistake to consider their job simplistic. A football ball boy must possess an instinctive type of intelligence that is no less masterful than their tennis counterparts and can impact a game in a way possible in no other sport. They also often have a flair for cunning and trickery that only a footballing brain can have.

When a ball leaves the football pitch everything is suspended, but only momentarily. The clock continues and play resumes as soon as it re-enters the field by either a throw-in or a goal kick. This means that much importance is often placed on the speed at which the ball ends up back on the pitch. A quickly retrieved ball can allow a team to continue the momentum of their attack before the defending team has a chance to gather themselves, and can be crucial in piling on pressure against an opponent. Whereas a ball that finds its way back onto the field of play minutes after it leaves can effectively stop a team in its tracks and is ideal for a team attempting to kill the momentum of a game. The difference in timing so often comes down to the ball boy.

Ball boys are effectively a metronome influencing the pace of play. Provided by the home team, and selected from local schools, youth leagues or fan clubs, they are also often heavily biased. There are few people more fanatical than a football-mad child, and when placed in a situation where they can actively shape the fortunes of their

Toronto Blue Jays versus Baltimore Orioles, 19 May 2017

beloved team, the urge to intervene some-times proves too great. Football ball boys can regularly be seen throwing balls away from players, outrageously wasting time and even heckling. And although clubs deny they actively encourage this behaviour, they don't seem particularly concerned about stamping it out. It is this lack of impartiality that makes them such a force.

Perhaps the most infamous ball boying incident in recent memory, and one that perfectly demonstrates their capacity to influence a game, occurred when Chelsea player Eden Hazard was sent off during the 2013 Capital One Cup semi-final match against Swansea for appearing to kick a ball boy in the ribs after he had purposefully smothered the ball. Chelsea went on to lose without their star player and Swansea went on to the final where they eventually won the cup. Managers José Mourinho and Pep Guardiola, of Manchester United and Manchester City respectively, have even incorporated ball boys into their tactical masterplans. The latter having instructed his ball boys to speed up the return of the ball in certain phases of play to create an

atmosphere of relentless attack and the former having sacked all his ball boys and replaced them with youth academy players whom he deemed better able to read the nuances of a competitive game.

ALL-AMERICAN BALL BOYS

The role of the ball boy in American sports is more of a profession than an endeavour for brave schoolchildren. The American ball boy sits somewhere between a regular ball boy and a full-time locker room attendant. It's typically a low-paying job but it's a job nonetheless, with a career progression that, if you are good enough, allows you to progress to an equipment manager role, overseeing all kit-related matters.

Rather than spectacular feats on and around the field of play, American ball boys are perhaps more notable for their intimate relationship with the ball, which goes hand in hand with a wider attitude in American sport culture. The three biggest team sports played in America (basketball, baseball and American football) all share a distinctly fetishistic attitude towards the balls they use. Tennis players simply require a fresh supply throughout play, while football is far more concerned with the new; with each season bringing a brand-new design of ball for players to kick and, most importantly, for consumers to buy. (Over the past decade a new and improved — always 'improved' — model of Nike ball has been used in each season of the Premier League.) In contrast, American sports are wedded to the idea of the ball as a continuum. Something considered near perfect that, rather than being continually upgraded and replaced each season, should be maintained to precise specifications. Tradition and craft take precedence over technological advancement.

Wilson Sporting Goods has been the NFL ball supplier for over 75 years, while the Horween Leather Company has been the sole tanner and leather maker for NFL footballs since the 1940s. Basketballs are a similar cottage industry, with Spalding having been the sole provider of NBA game balls since 1983 and Horween Leather also serving as the leather provider: always producing eight panels of leather around a rubber sphere. There was a single deviation in the 2006–7 season when Spalding introduced a newly designed ball with different shaped panels made from a microfiber composite. It was the first time in 35 years that the ball had been changed, and so great was the uproar from players that the new design was scrapped halfway through the season and regular leather balls reintroduced.

Only one company (Rawlings) supplies baseballs to the MLB, and there is only one factory in the world, located in Costa Rica, authorized to make them. Every single ball is made by hand out of white cowhide with exactly 108 stitches of red New Zealand wool yarn sewn in a figure-8 pattern.

This fastidiousness is understandable given that each sport involves the precise movement of a ball through the air by someone shooting, passing or pitching, often at great speed and distance — the tiniest alteration to a ball or a player's experience handling it can make a huge difference.

To get a ball 'just right', a level of ritualism is employed that often borders on voodoo-like and the help of ball boys is

The modern-day tennis ball boy is the most rigorously drilled in the world of sport

often enlisted. Superstitions, secretive treatments and strange substances abound. Basketballs, for example, are not just ready to play with straight from the factory. At the Spalding headquarters each ball is placed into a catapult machine and fired repeatedly, fifty or so times, at a hardwood floor to begin 'breaking in' the ball. Then a quota of balls for the season, usually 72, are sent to teams in the summer where they start getting used in training sessions. It is the sweat and oils from human hands that are said to be the final, crucial, step to breaking a ball in and softening the leather. Ball boys are often tasked with trying to keep favoured balls in circulation and players will often mark them with little symbols to help tell a good ball from a dud.

In baseball, meanwhile, every single ball used in an MLB game will have been rubbed by a ball boy or an equipment manager sitting in a small room with a jar of mud. Each pot of the mysterious dirt (called 'Lena Blackburne Baseball Rubbing Mud') is sourced from the same secret location somewhere on the banks of the Delaware river and is said to add friction to

Cincinnati Reds versus Florida Gators, 18 March, 2012

the ball and aid a pitcher's grip. Meanwhile the continual chucking of foul balls into the crowd by ball boys during baseball games is not just part of the spectacle. So great is the effect of any nick or scuff on the flight of a pitch that, for purposes of consistency, balls are changed as soon as one hits a bat or the floor. A ball often lasts no more than two pitches and baseball teams can use upwards of one hundred baseballs in a single game, with the entirety of the MLB using almost one million balls in a season. It is worth noting that this is only a fairly recent development with the advent of foreign labour and cheaper means of production. The relatively low-scoring period between 1900 and 1919 is known as the 'Dead-ball Era', when the then more expensive balls were kept in use for so long that they grew mangled and discoloured, meaning batters struggled to hit, or even see, anything.

Perhaps the greatest ball obsessives are found in American football, along with the most intimate interaction between ball boy and ball. The primary method of distribution on an American football field is via a pinpoint accurate pass launched into the hands of a running teammate. The correct feel and comfort of a ball is so important for accurate passing that an NFL quarterback won't even consider using one until it has been thoroughly broken in to his own specifications. Much like basketball, each team receives their quota of balls at the beginning of pre-season. A team of ball boys, and often senior equipment managers, will work for days at a time, taking the new balls and rubbing, soaking, scouring and sanding them over and over again until the smell of leather fills their nostrils and the balls are thoroughly worn in to the exact preference of their quarterbacks. During subsequent practice sessions the very best balls are identified for use in competitive games, upon which they are set aside and guarded as though they were jewels for the entirety of the season.

21ST-CENTURY BALL BOYS

While ball boys do remain peripheral figures in sport, particularly when compared to the millionaire athletes they serve, something is changing. Ball boys are becoming increasingly visible. This is due in part to the shifting way in which we watch and consume sport. We have never had access to more leagues and more games at such a global scale. It is possible to tune into a soccer match in Saudi Arabia, a Swiss tennis tournament, or a Friday night baseball game somewhere in the American Midwest.

There are more cameras, and camera angles, than ever before, not to mention the do-it-yourself broadcasters sharing notable moments on their iPhones. Nothing goes unnoticed and there's nothing that can't be packaged into a video clip and shared online instantaneously. This is coincidentally opening up a new level of appreciation for the ball boy and a new opportunity to see them in action that wouldn't necessarily be afforded through traditional sports broadcasting.

Some have even become breakout stars, with red-haired Florida State University ball boy Frankie Grizzle-Malgrat (a.k.a. Red Lightning) becoming such a sensation that he earned a call-up to the NFL, joining the Atlanta Falcons as their ball boy. While quick-thinking Fernanda Maia from Brazil was filmed setting up a goal for her home team with a speedy return of the ball. She was awarded an assist by the newspapers and the somewhat creepy offer of a modelling contract with Brazilian Playboy. She currently works as a football pundit on Brazilian television.

More often than not, ball boys provide light relief. As though they've never been able to shake the echoes of two small boys standing behind a fat man one Saturday afternoon in London. They are typically celebrated for moments of genius (an incredible catch, ball control, an amazing assist), or, more likely, just by doing inadvertently funny things (falling over, embarrassing players, embarrassing themselves, getting hit by balls). The sheer volume of 'ball boy fails', 'ball boy skills', 'ball boy funny moments' compilations on YouTube attest to their now-established popularity in sporting subculture. An argument could be made for them being easily the most sung-about of sport's 'unsung heroes'.

A cohesive ball boy machine should be almost imperceptible to spectators

There is more opportunity than ever to ponder over the incidental and unusual moments in sport, and ball boys are the perfect subject for this new gaze. It's like glimpsing the inner workings of a machine that one shouldn't otherwise be able to see — a reassuring human figure to laugh at and to cheer for in the midst of superstars.

TENNIS

Work in groups of six, each with a specific position on the court. Two 'centres' stay bent down at either side of the net, ready to rush past and gather any netted balls. These individuals are usually smaller and quicker, best suited to the continual crouching and dashing. A further four ball boys, called 'bases', are positioned one in each corner of the court. This role is typically taken on by the taller kids, who receive balls from the 'centres' and make sure the player at their end receives any balls, towels, or water they may require. Each position has a specific code to accompany it. 'RB1', for example, being the 'base' ball boy on the right-hand side of the umpire and on the near side of court.

FOOTBALL

Usually found lying in wait just in front of or behind the advertising hoarding. Space themselves out at regular intervals, including by the corner flags and behind the goals. In major competitions such as the Champions League or World Cup, they often wear special bibs to make themselves easily noticeable by players. Often just out of camera shot when a game is broadcast, their presence confirmed by a ball suddenly flying back into the field of play from off-screen or a player gesticulating frantically to speed up slow service.

BASEBALL

Can be found crouched on stools behind both of the foul-lines — the two diagonal white lines running out left and right from the batter's box. It is their duty to snatch up any foul shots that may come their way. They are part miraculous shot-stopper, part crowd-pleaser, often flying through the air, to catch a ball in mid-flight just before it goes crashing into the face of a spectator. Also spend large amounts of time chatting with the crowd and help with 'shagging', which sounds rude if you are British but is not too dissimilar from 'rebounding' in basketball in that a batter will practice whacking shots out into the field and the ball boy will help to gather up and return the balls.

BASKETBALL

Notable for hardly having any in-game involvement with the ball. Because the sport is played in such an intimate arena, with the court completely surrounded by fans, staff, coaches and players, it doesn't take much to get the ball back into play. Do help to time save during training, where they will 'rebound' (standing under or around the net to collect and return the ball) for players doing shooting practice. Much of their role involves locker room duties like providing ice packs and towels, making sure everyone's training kits are folded, and even running errands for players, going on food runs to restaurants or getting phone numbers from attractive fans. Earn very little but make the majority of their income through tips from players and referees (whom they also help). It's a uniquely American blend of sport and service culture. Have an important in-game duty to clean up any water or sweat spillages — which are particularly dangerous on the hardwood floor. They can often be seen running onto the court with rags and mops after a water break or if a particularly sweaty player takes a tumble.

AMERICAN FOOTBALL

Charge up and down the length of the field, following play. Their role is to provide a ball at the beginning of each new attacking phase of play and to minimize delay. There are different levels of ball boy, with many of them simply there to provide water, towels and whatever else a player might need — a more sinister rumour is that some carry vials of smelling salts to help revive players who have just been in a crunching tackle. A select few are responsible for handling the balls throughout the game. They are easily identifiable by their special vests, with a large red 'X' on the front and back and a handy marsupial-like pouch on the stomach for storing extra balls.

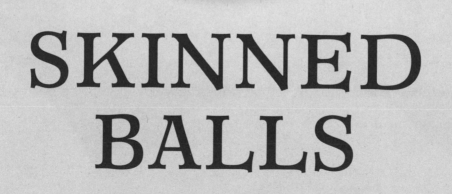

SKINNED
BALLS

Art Direction by MacGuffin   Photography by Mathijs Labadie

Top Glider, Telstar 18, Adidas, Match Ball Replica, size 5, 2018 FIFA World Cup Russia, Made in China, 2018

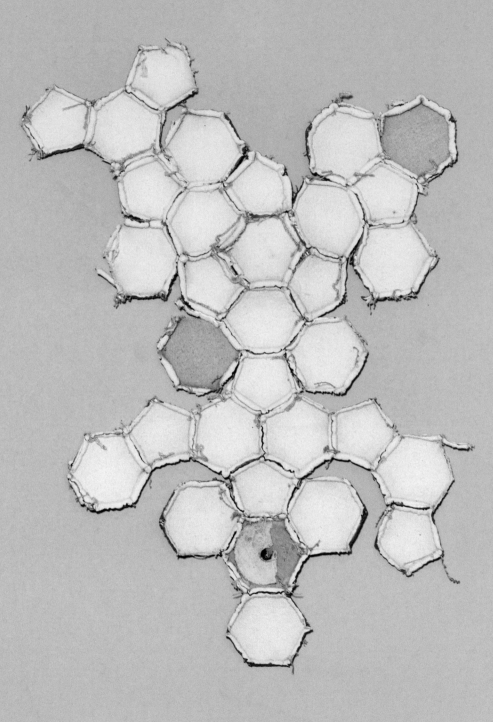

Beach, E&L Sports, Made in Pakistan, 2018

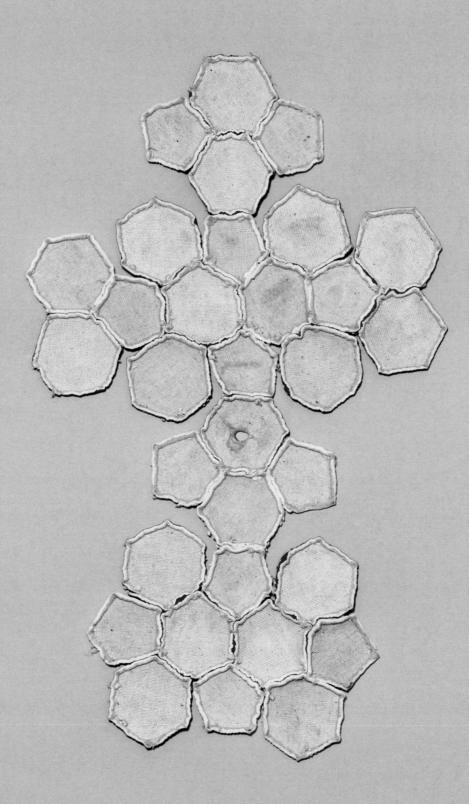

Roteiro Mini, Adidas, UEFA Official Match Ball Replica, origin unknown, 2004

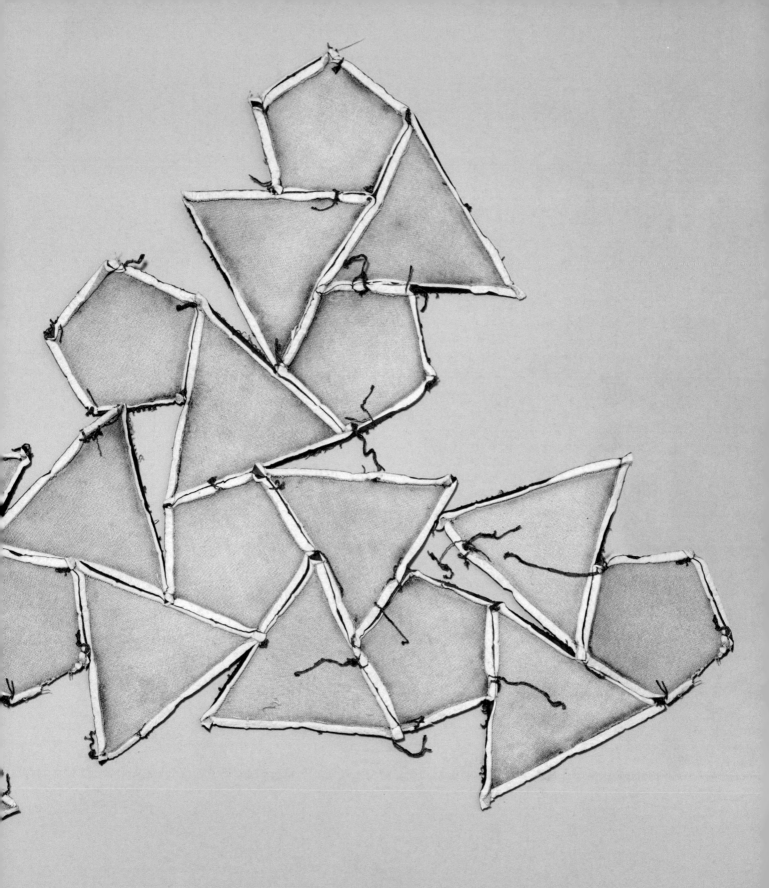

Unknown ball

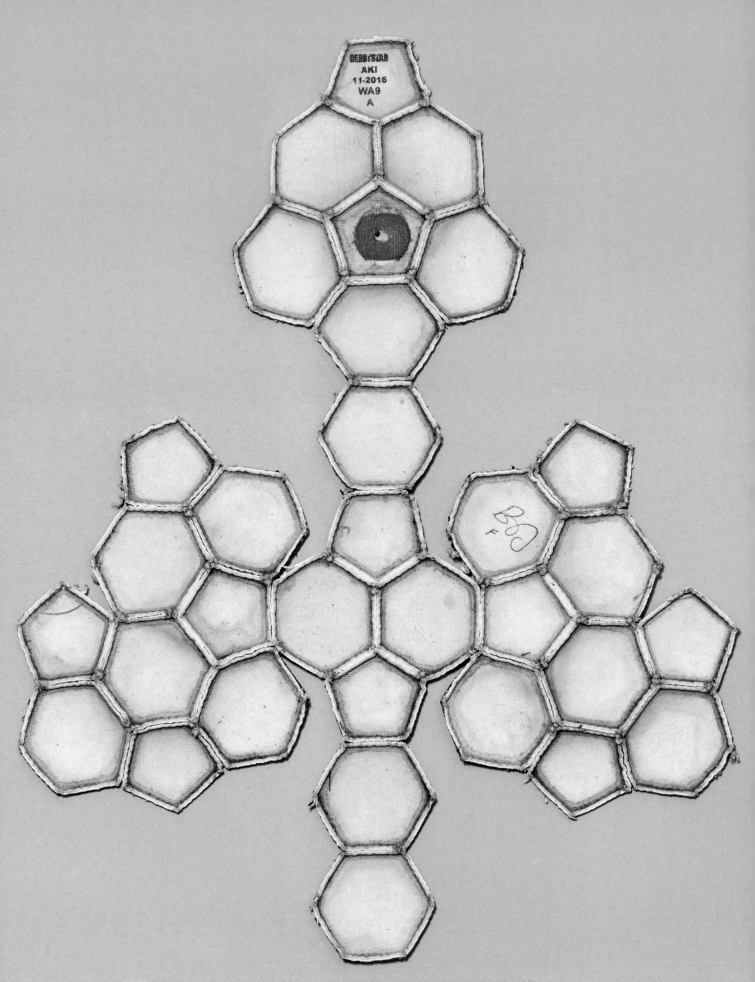

Players Number 88, Derbystar, International Match Standard, origin unknown, 2016

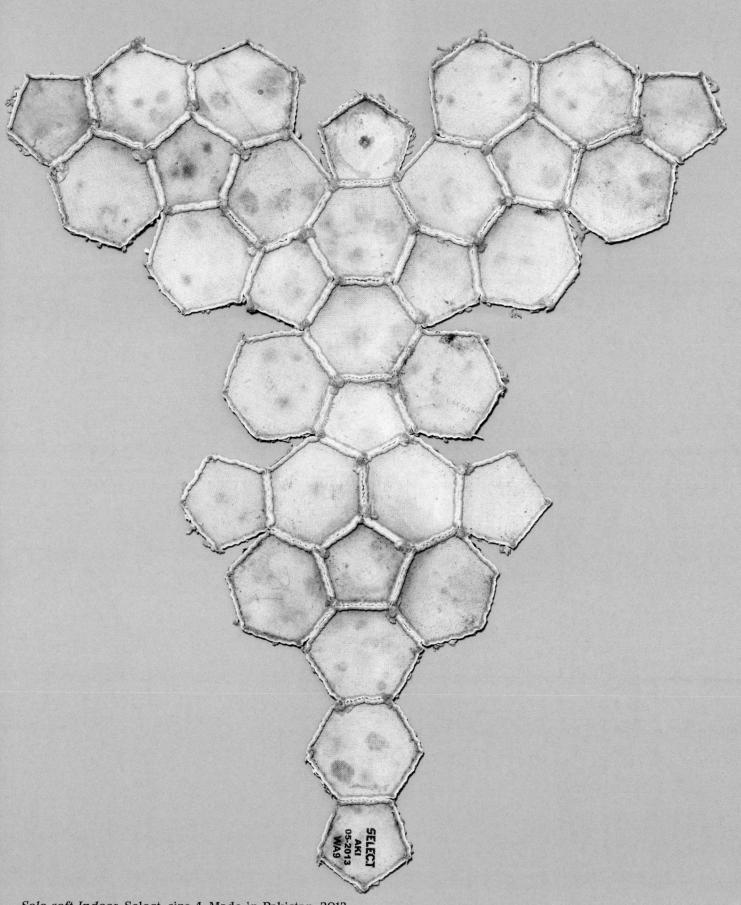

Solo soft Indoor, Select, size 4, Made in Pakistan, 2013

Ajax Briljant Replica Ball, Derbystar, Made in Germany, 1997

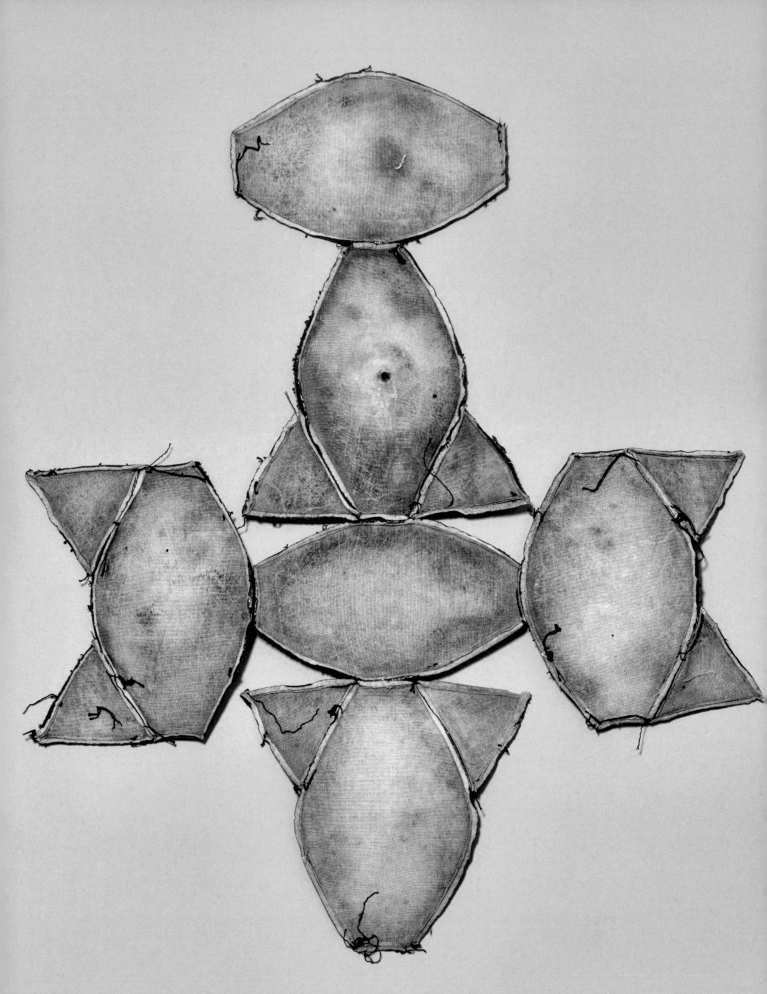

Adidas, origin and date unknown

Adi Pure, Glider Soccer Ball, Adidas, size 5, origin unknown, 2010

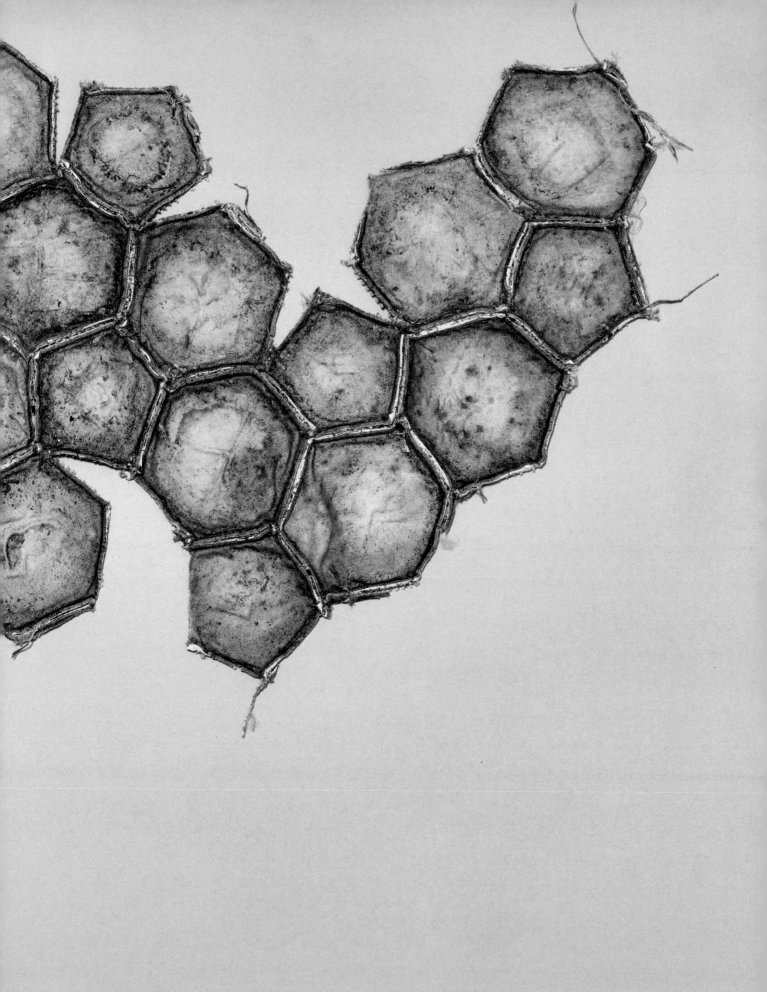

Champion, E&L Sports, E&L Sports, size 5, 320 grams, Made in China, 2013

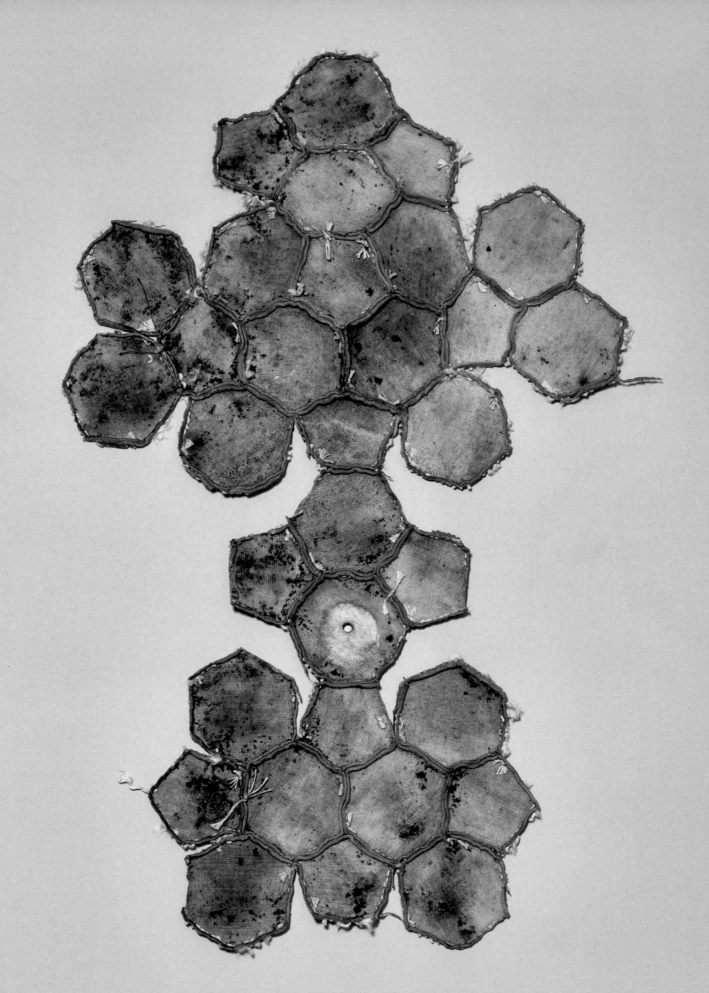

E.K 2004, Bastion Hotels, Made in China, 2004

Supreme, E&L Sports, origin unknown, 2015

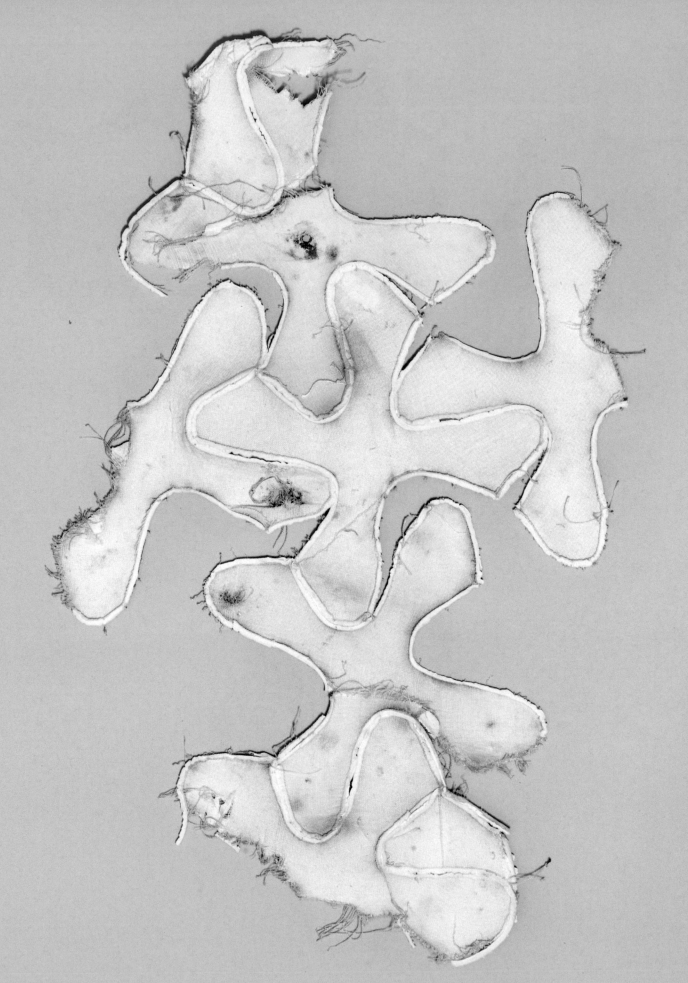

Euro 2016 'Beau Jeu', Adidas, UEFA Official Match Ball Replica, origin unknown, 2016

1930   T-MODEL

(Uruguay) 12 T-shaped panels and a lace to inflate the bladder

1934   FEDERALE 102

(Italy) 13 leather panels, manufactured in Italy by order of the Mussolini regime

1938   ALLEN

(France) ball with a cotton lining, named after the manufacturer

1950   DUPLO T

(Brazil) the first sealed ball, with no lace but with a valve

1954 SWISS WORLD CHAMPION

(Switzerland) with striking zig-zag edges which, like all the balls at that time, are hand sewn

1958   TOP STAR

(Sweden) ball with a waterproof waxed surface, made by the Swedish *Sydsvenska Laderoch Remfabriken*

1962   CRACK

(Chile) unique for its 18 irregular polygonal panels

1966   CHALLENGE

(England) orange leather ball with 25 rectangular panels, selected after a blind football test

1970   TELSTAR

(Mexico) the first ball by Adidas, with 32 black and white leather panels to be easily visible on TV

1974   TELSTAR DURLAST

(West Germany) a remake of the 1970 Telstar, now also with an all-orange and all-white version for use in the dark

1978   TANGO

(Argentina) ball with a triangular design that looks extremely cool in motion—hence its name

BALL BEHAVIOUR

Football is the world's most popular sport, with an emotional impact that borders on hysteria. Psychologists have determined that the excitement of a football match is equivalent to that of extreme emotional situations, such as having a child, getting fired or falling in love. Add to that the enormous financial interests and nationalism that comes with a world championship and it is no wonder that all aspects of a World Cup match — from the referees to the design of the ball — are meticulously weighed up against the motto 'Fair Play'.

Until 1970, World Cup football matches were played with whatever ball was produced locally. In 1966 in England, for example, that was an orange leather ball by the British Slazenger Company, the *Challenge*. The 18-panel ball was selected in a blind test at the Football Association Headquarters on Soho Square in London, but in the tournament, it was also alternated, when convenient, with white or brown balls by other manufacturers. To deal with the problem of dissimilar balls once and for all, in 1968 the Féderation Internationale de Football Association (FIFA) commissioned Adidas to develop a universal competition ball. The resulting *Telstar* (named after the communication satellite that broadcast the football matches at that time) was the first official FIFA ball, introduced for the 1970 World Cup in Mexico. The ball had twelve black pentagons and twenty white hexagons, thus making it clearly visible on a black and white TV. Although made of leather, it was still water-resistant to some extent due to a shiny layer of paint. The *Telstar* set the standard for an entire generation of World Cup balls.

Since the Mexico World Cup in 1970, Adidas paid FIFA huge sums of money every four years to be the sole official supplier of the World Cup ball. And every four years that led to discussions about underweight, overweight, erratic, drifting or uncontrollable balls. The *Fevernova* ball, which was used in South Korea in 2002 and was lighter than previous balls, was regarded as a ball that would benefit the more technical players. 'A ridiculous kiddie's bouncing ball,' said the Italian goalkeeper Gianluigi Buffon. In 2006 the German goalkeeper Oliver Kahn claimed that the heavier *Teamgeist* ball 'was built in favour of the strikers'. Virtually all the players at the 2010 World Cup in South Africa hated the *Jabulani* ball because of its unpredictable movement. 'It behaves like a f*cking beach ball,' said the Spanish team.

You might think that it's not that difficult to make a ball. To create the same conditions for each player and each match, the ball must be as round and durable as possible. In addition, it must absorb as little water as possible during the match to avoid changes in weight. On the drawing board, the design of such

1982 TANGO ESPANA

(Spain) leather ball with a polyurethane coating, which makes it far less likely to absorb water

1986 AZTECA

(Mexico) the first fully synthetic ball with an Aztec pattern design

1990 ETRUSCO UNICO

(Italy) remake of the Tango & Azteca, now with 'Etruscan' patterns

1994 QUESTRA

(United States) remake of the previous three balls, now with 'Interstellar' patterns to mark the 25th anniversary of the Apollo 11 mission

1998 TRICOLORE

(France) the first multicoloured ball, produced outside Europe in Morocco

2002 FEVERNOVA

(South Korea & Japan) ball with an interior of syntactic foam to decrease weight

2006 TEAMGEIST

(Germany) the first fully waterproof ball, because its seams are heat sealed rather than sewn

2010 JABULANI

(South Africa) according to measurements the roundest, and to users the most erratic, ball ever

2014 BRAZUCA

(Brazil) ball with just six panels and a surface with tiny bumps, intended to improve the grip and consistency

2018 TELSTAR 18

(Russia) ball with six textured panels and a chip with which it can be located using an app

a ball is not a problem, but to actually achieve the desired characteristics is a different story. The seams of the ball prove to be the biggest problem. After the 2010 World Cup, NASA studied the controversial *Jabulani* ball: 'Knuckling occurs when, at zero or near-zero spin, the seams of the ball channel airflow in an unusual and erratic manner making its trajectory unpredictable.' The criticasters of the various balls often talk about their unnatural weight, but in reality, the weight of the balls does not vary much — both the *Teamgeist* and the *Jabulani* are 420 grams, while the maximum weight under FIFA's rules is 445 grams. According to the experts, however, it is not about the *Teamgeist* and *Jabulani* having a different weight or fewer panels than the Telstar, but the fact that they have fewer seams. A football with 32 panels has a seam length of about 405 cm, the *Teamgeist* has 345 and the *Jabulani* 203. It is not the weight, but the seams that determine the controllability of the ball.

Furthermore, the heat-sealed seams of the balls after 1974 are much shallower than the traditional, stitched football. A laser scan of the surface of the *Jabulani* and a stitched ball from the NASA study shows that the stitched seam is twice as deep as that of the heat-sealed ball. 'The floating, beach ball-like behaviour of these footballs isn't because they are light,' according to football researcher Simon Choppin, 'but because they are smooth.' That is due to a complicated process of low pressure and traction. In short, the air flowing over the ball causes a low-pressure area behind it — a wake. This wake creates a tractive force and thus slows the ball. Crucially, the seams of a football disturb the air, helping it to enter 'low drag' at lower speeds. A perfectly smooth football would be unplayable; high levels of drag would radically alter the behaviour of the ball. This is why the increased smoothness of the 2010 *Jabulani* ball made it less stable.

As if the controversy had been anticipated beforehand, Adidas chose the slogan 'Love me or Loose Me' for the radically differ-

ent design of the *Brazuca* ball in 2014. Scientists at least loved the ball. 'It is more stable in flight and will handle more like a traditional 32-panel ball,' said Dr Rabi Mehta of the NASA Ames Research Center. Although the ball had fewer sections than its predecessor, it achieved a much longer seam length due to its finger-like panels. The seams were also deeper than those of the Jabulani, and the surface of the ball had small bumps. That roughness and the new panel configuration had a positive influence on the handling of the *Brazuca*, according to Dr Mehta: 'There is a thin layer of air that forms near the ball's surface called the boundary layer, and it is the state and behaviour of that layer that is critical to the performance of the ball. The materials used, the ball's surface roughness and its distribution determines its aerodynamics. The players will enjoy the new ball.' Portugal striker Cristiano Ronaldo was not one of those players at the 2014 World Cup. 'It drifts. And I already drift myself; then you get a double drift. Before you know it, the ball drifts out of the stadium.'

For the 2018 World Cup in Russia, Adidas reverted to the 1970 *Telstar* model. However, unlike in 1970, the *Telstar 18* ball has 18 panels instead of 32 and the seams are glued. The main innovation is the addition of a microchip, which allows the ball to 'communicate' with its owner via a smartphone. Despite the chip and the new design, which according to Adidas is 'scientific', 'predictable' and was tested for two years in wind tunnels, the ball did not meet all the expectations during the tournament. Two *Telstar 18*'s burst during the Australia–France match, and the ball deflated very slowly in the Saudi Arabia–Uruguay game. International keepers were also less than enthusiastic. Spanish keepers Pepe Reina and David de Gea complained that the ball could be slippery due to the smooth coating and lack of seams and that it changed direction unpredictably. 'Luckily,' said the Russian TV station Russia 24, 'you can always find the ball again with your smartphone when it drifts away.'

KA

BLOWIN' IN THE WIND

Nothing quite captures the spirit of freedom and life in the great outdoors like the humble tumbleweed, though the best place to study it is indoors, on the shelves of the Royal Botanic Gardens in Kew, London.

STILL FROM *THE TUMBLEWEED TRAINER*, BROTHERS & SISTERS FOR PEARL & DEAN, 2016

Text by Lindsay Sekulowicz

Tumbleweeds pile up in Clovis, USA. Photo Alamy

Make them like tumbleweed, my God, like chaff before the wind. As fire consumes the forest or a flame sets the mountains ablaze, so pursue them with your tempest and terrify them with your storm. Cover their faces with shame, Lord, so that they will seek your name. — Psalm 83

Tumbleweeds, the iconic rolling spheres of the plant kingdom, have meandered across cinema screens and barren wastelands of our cultural consciousness to become synonymous with destitution and alienation from society. Yet through time, as both plants and people have migrated, many tumbleweeds have taken on great significance across many cultures and religions. And not only do they have a remarkable botanical diversity, but a more lucid examination demonstrates their practical and medicinal uses across the centuries and reveals the changeable nature of their relationship to their human neighbours.

In a study of the connections between people and plants, the Economic Botany Collection at the Royal Botanic Gardens, Kew, is a treasure chest in which to begin. This is a 100,000 strong collection, comprised of raw plant materials and artefacts that represent the entire extent of the human use of plants around the world — from medicines to food, musical instruments, toys, textiles, dyes, and every other organic possibility in between. Looking for tumbleweeds in here, one uncovers countless other balls along the way: balls of twine, rubber balls, blue balls of pressed indigo and woad, early golf balls and bowling balls, balls of tobacco and trays for holding opium balls. There is a giant, rounded puffball mushroom held in plastic wrapping that looks as if it might implode at a glancing touch, and there are wooden models of cauliflowers, Brussel sprouts, radishes and a dozen varieties of apples. Inside one box is an enormous ball made out of popcorn — a failed glitterball in stale yellow. Who made this thing and how did it end up here? Of the items on these shelves, where continents can be traversed within an arm's reach and where objects and stories picked by some wind or whim, it is fitting that tumbleweeds are the balls to be examined here. For these are the ones that

move most freely, unrestrained by roots and soil, and mirror the manner in which thoughts and stories roam so easily in here.

Botanically speaking, a tumbleweed is not one particular species but rather a name given after a plant's method of seed dispersal. These are just plants, or parts of plants, that roll — those that habitually break away from their roots and are driven by the wind to turn and spin, anywhere the environment is open and they can travel freely without obstruction or interruption from forests or mountains. This is usually across deserts, though they have also been known to travel unwelcomed in great numbers through towns and allegedly even overseas.

Many examples of tumbleweeds that have crossed the paths of people are held within the collections at Kew Gardens. Among these, *Kali tragus** is certainly the one we think of first, rolling across the sandy streets between bars and sheriffs' offices in every Western film that has been made. These are the great metaphorical punctuators of bad jokes, and that tiny bouncing Skype emoji that no-one uses anymore because we are all almost constantly connected. In tumbleweed terms, they are huge — up to a metre in diameter, inedible to most livestock, and a fire hazard when accumulating in any large quantity. A single large specimen can produce up to 200,000 seeds. This size and rate of growth can occasionally cause significant damage. In 2014, the town of Clovis in New Mexico was devoured by these prickly globes — they began to arrive on a Sunday and continued over the coming days as a steady ocean, or as one resident stated, 'like a heard of cows' that piled up to ten feet tall and necessitated military equipment to evacuate people from their homes. In the 1980s, there was an experimental attempt funded by the Arizona Solar Energy Research Commission and the US Department of Energy to commercialize the weed. This involved the manufacture of 'tumblelogs', made by passing tumbleweeds through hammermills to make a coarse flour that was compacted into slow-burning logs to create a renewable and local fuel source. In the storerooms at Kew, we are led back to Kali tragus' native Eurasia, where the tumblelog with its graphic American 1980s Deco packaging sits alongside a jar of the charred roots of the plant, collected in Iraq almost 150 years before, where the alkali (the name coming from the Arabic, *Al-Qaly* meaning 'from the ashes') that was extracted from these roots would have been a useful commodity.

Solanum rostratum

Another pestilent tumbleweed is *Solanum rostratum*, a spiny nightshade pollinated by bees. This is the ancestral host to the Colorado potato beetle, one of the most prolific agricultural pests in history. During the Cold War it was even claimed that the CIA had introduced the insect into Russia to interrupt food security. The week before Charles Darwin died, he had placed an order of *Solanum rostratum* seeds, though this was for a separate study of pollination strategies rather than for any subversive plot.

Aristida funiculata

Other tumbleweeds in the storerooms are fascinating simply for the mechanics of their movement: There is a whole shelf filled with dense bundles of *Aristida funiculata* from Sudan. On one, a label reads:

This specimen was sent by Dr Pettet from Khartoum. It consists of the awned fruits of Aristida funiculata, which once emerged as small balls, are blown along by the wind and expand as more awns become entangled. This specimen has become too heavy to be rolled along by the wind and probably skidded along on one side where it has become abraded.

Misshapen by the wind, the ground and their own weight, with seeds snapped off at the ends, these beautiful tumbleweeds still seem unbelievably clean and unscathed by their journeys through the Sudanese desert.

Brunsvigia bosmaniae

Often, the visceral smell and colour of a plant is lost here over time, replaced by the uniform soft rusts of the herbarium colour palette. *Brunsvigia bosmaniae* grows across dry grasslands and rocky outcrops of the Western Cape in South Africa. It flowers after the summer rains have ended, filling the land with fields of hot pink pompom blooms with an intense scent that increases at night-time, when they are pollinated by hawkmoths. These plants are generally poisonous and therefore avoided by animals, so once the seeds are ripe, the stems dry and then they break off at the ground, leaving a perfect circle of umbrella stalks that travel until they are slowed down, lamed by the detachment of their seed 'feet' which germinate rapidly where they land.

Selaginella lepidophylla

In all these species, the plant in its tumble-weed form is dead, though this is a functional death because the plant needs to degrade in order to let the seeds escape and hopefully land in an optimum place to grow. In certain other species, though, if the tumbleweed stops in a wet location, and the time and season is right, the plant will begin to swell as moisture flows back into the dry fronds and the seeds emerge from new life in the plant. *Selaginella lepidophylla* is the 'false rose of Jericho', a plant native to Mexico, which can survive in a state of almost complete desiccation until it is exposed to only the slightest amount of water, whereby the leaves become green again. Early Spanish missionaries used this plant to demonstrate ideas of resurrection and rebirth in their conversions. The plant has some medicinal qualities too and is used as an infusion for treating colds and flu. For even more fascinating medicinal properties, however, we can look to the true Rose of Jericho, *Anastatica hierochuntica*, a plant native to arid regions of the Middle East and North Africa. It has many other names, but among the most appropriate are 'Hand of Mary', 'Maryam's flower' and 'Kaff Maryam' — titles given after the most revered of women and the only woman named in the Quran. For these tiny sturdy wicker balls have been historically used across the Middle East as a medicine for infertility, pain relief in pregnancy and childbirth, and for antimicrobial and antioxidant properties in postnatal care.

    Anastatica hierochuntica can be found in dry and stony places with elevations above 3,000 feet. At the end of the rainy season, the plant drops its leaves and curls its branches into a tight ball to hibernate and wait for the next rainfall. Within this ball, the fruits remain attached and closed to protect the seeds, which are very hardy and

can remain dormant for years, until exposure to rain, when they are released and able to germinate within a matter of hours. When consumed, the entire plant is used, usually placed in water to expand, with the resulting infusion drunk by the cupful. In her 2007 film *Kaff Mariam*, the artist Anna Lucas traced a journey of the plant, beginning in a herbalist shop in Brixton Market in South London, back through Palestine to the Sinai desert. Beautiful slow-panning scenes reveal glimpses of globalization occurring within the remote regions where she travels, and show local and indigenous knowledge practices against a backdrop of political concern that was particularly poignant at that time.

Anastatica hierochuntica

Considering all these tumbleweeds and numerous associations, is it perhaps this idea of the borderless migration of *Anastatica hierochuntica* that is the most significant. As we opened with a biblical lament, provoked by the threat of an invasion of Israel by its Assyrian neighbours, we are urged by an unnamed narrator to recognize ultimate power. Yet the idea of the tumbleweed being scattered would be the least optimistic metaphor of struggle and conflict we could create, and instead we can overwrite this with these small and resilient tumbleweeds that continue their natural spread in these same regions where free travel has become so restricted. Many cultures still identify with the use of this plant, and see it as a sign of new life and growth. We could regard these tumbling orbs as representational of our own migrations and stories, and the rolling, and natural passing of knowledge over time.

Kali tragus, the great cinematic tumbleweed, has long travelled across our screens without origin or end, punctuating empty landscapes, signifying impeding storms and acting as a silent countdown for the classic cowboy showdown. They have appeared in everything from *Beetlejuice* to *The Simpsons*, flying through the air in *The Wizard of Oz* shortly before Dorothy is caught in a terrifying tornado, forming the slow opening (over a cliff edge, across a bridge and past taco stands) of *The Big Lebowski*, and littering the path of a wagon in *Giant* as Elizabeth Taylor and Rock Hudson gaze at each other inside; and it is in these classic Western roles that we know them best.

Far from being a quintessentially American phenomenon however, *Kali tragus* is actually a highly invasive species from Eurasia, also known as Russian thistle, and was accidentally introduced into North America in the late 19th century by way of flaxseed imports from Russia. To continue the idea of cultural migration then, it turns out that some of the greatest ever Westerns were shot outside the USA. In the 1960s and 1970s, the Tabernas Desert in southern Spain became a popular Hollywood outpost, and Sergio Leone's *The Good, the Bad and the Ugly* and *Once Upon a Time in the West* were among many films shot there. But still, this not-so-American weed epitomizes everything that we think we know about this genre with a kind of botanical nostalgia, worded perfectly by William S. Hart, producer and star of the 1925 silent film *Tumbleweeds*, who said of his business:

My friends, I loved the art of making motion pictures. It is as the breath of life to me... the rush of the wind that cuts your face, the pounding hooves of the pursuing posse, and then the clouds of dust! Through the cloud of dust comes the faint voice of the director, 'Now, Bill, OK! Glad you made it! Great stuff, Bill, great stuff! And, say, Bill! Give old Fritz a pat on the nose for me, will ya?' The saddle is empty, the boys up ahead are calling, they're waiting for you and me to help drive this last great round-up into eternity.

The Last Picture Show, 1971

800 Bullets, 2002

Silverado, 1985

Giant, 1956

Streets of Laredo, 1995

Arizona Dream, 1992

The Wizard of Oz, 1939

Wicked, 1998

Scarecrow, 1973

Tumbleweeds, 1925

Chuck Versus the Bearded Bandit, 2011

The Simpsons, 2009

Gerry, 2002

Man in the Saddle, 1951

Dead Like Me: The Bycicle Thief, 2003

Giant, 1956

Married With Children, 1993

The Plainsman, 1936

Rango, 2011

Resident Evil: Extinction, 2007

Gunsmoke, 1955

Last Man Standing, 1996

An American Tail: Fievel Goes West, 1991

Tumbleweeds, 1999

The Big Lebowski, 1998

AN IMPASSIVE BALL

A story by . . . . Adania Shibli
Drawings by . . . . Fahri

I   AN IMPASSIVE BALL

The war, it seemed, was over, after it had
reached the far extremes of violence. In short,
it had reached a peak, and here were the
soldiers packing away their possessions and
collecting their equipment, tired, exhausted,
and spent, having given all their energy
to battle. Therefore they went on tossing
everything without much care, into their kit
bags and vehicles. There were vehicles for
carrying the troops, then others for carrying
military equipment, for the crates of bullets
and grenades, for transporting tanks, and
for the tins of food, some past their expiry
date. As far as the eye could see, these were
the only things that had survived undamaged.
Buildings all around, however, had been
shelled and were now riddled with haphazard
holes, lumps of them dropped onto the streets
and pavements, and paint peeled from their
facades and interior walls, which still surrounded the furniture that those fleeing the
bombardment had been unable to carry with
them. Less visible were the corpses of all
ages scattered around the place. Or, maybe
more accurately, they should remain invisible.
Instead, focus should be limited to their
numbers, and if there were enough time,

II   AN IMPASSIVE BALL

it would be possible to mention their names
and ages, then the circumstances of their
deaths, including what they were doing at the
instant they were killed, and what they would
nevermore be able to do. Except this would
be an arduous task. In fact, it would be nearly
impossible to gather all this information,
which would most likely be forgotten at the
nearest available opportunity, regardless of
the considerable amount of sympathy, even
sadness, it may elicit. Nothing of the sort
will be done here, though, eliminating the
possibility of this text being read as political
propaganda that may provoke the ire of
certain readers, particularly those from the
ranks of the intellectual middle class. Anyway,
these bodies, if they mean anything to anyone,
other than those to whom they belonged, it
would be to those who were closest to them,
and perhaps their killers as well. Not now, but
later. Most likely, many years later, because
now these killers are tired, exhausted, and
spent, and are using whatever energy they
still have to collect their possessions and their
equipment, to leave this battlefield and get
back to their homes without delay. So they
must collect everything that has survived

undamaged or hasn't been used, and put it either in their kit bags or in the appropriate vehicle. And everything that has not survived or has been used, they must collect into huge garbage bags, a task which they perform without the care they give to collecting their possessions and equipment. Nevertheless, when they leave the place at last, they will leave some of it behind, and not only the garbage bags. In the meantime, distant voices will be heard, claiming that love and peace will triumph in the end, and medical teams will get ready to enter the place, followed by the international press, humanitarian aid convoys, and human rights organizations, and slipping in behind them, a group of mischievous, curious children. As soon as they're in, each group will go on searching the place for anything that might fall within the scope of their interests. No need here to spend too long going over these interests, since they are well known. Therefore the text will turn directly to that group of mischievous, curious children which this time numbered among its ranks Mohammad, Mounira, Moneim, Mazen, Maysoon, Mukhles and Maya, all of whose names, by sheer coincidence, begin with the

letter M. Apart from that, and although they were born to families with different economic and social backgrounds, they have one other, fundamental thing in common: poverty. Mounira was the eldest, but Mohammad was the strongest, and the pair led the group through the almost abandoned battlefield, with Maya, youngest and smallest, always at the rear.

Every age and size has its advantages and disadvantages, but Maya was currently experiencing the downside only. While other members of the group rifled the soldiers' refuse for wonderful, rare and valuable things, she was finding things that were plentiful and that nobody cared about, like empty sardine tins and bullet casings. She went on to collect them, tossing one away whenever she found another in better condition, keeping the shiniest and least battered, until, at last, she found a sardine tin with the lid only slightly peeled back, though it was totally empty. And Maya immediately began filling it with the little bullet casings she'd collected and kept. Slowly and carefully, she slotted them in one-by-one, until the tin was full of casings stacked widthwise, at right angles to the way the

sardines are usually arranged. Then, all of a sudden, shouts of surprise and admiration came from the group up ahead, who then started running, with Maya following after though she had no idea why, except that in the current circumstances she, like them, was driven by an instinct to stick together always, as much as possible.

They all ran until they came to an area clear of buildings and people, where they used to play during peacetimes. Mounira sat down, and Mohammad followed suit, while the others stood clustered around them. As silence reigned, Mounira took a disc-shaped metal tin from beneath her shirt. There was writing on it, which none of them could decipher, though they knew exactly what it was from the image beneath it. An image of dull green cucumbers. Mounira began wrestling to open the tin, while Mohammad gave his instructions on how to do that, before he soon intervened, pulling the tin from her hands. Not that this meant that Mounira lost control of the tin. Not at all. Meanwhile, drool had started to build up in the clamped mouths, swallowed back whenever the

dammed mass rose too high to breathe. They, for certain, did not think of themselves as extremely poor children, but tinned pickles were a rarity in their food basket or, for that matter, in the landscape of their daily lives. Sometimes they'd spot them in the refrigerators of newly married couples, or at a lunch or a dinner party. But to find them like this, while they were playing around, was unimaginable. The question now was how many pickles were in the tin, and the number that each would get. There must be at least seven in there. Ten, perhaps. And it would be acceptable by everybody that Mounira and Mohammad, who'd found the tin, got the biggest and the most once the rest of them had been evenly divided, with the smallest pickle going to Maya. Her body, being the smallest and the youngest, did not really need so many. These thoughts, inner wonderings and imaginings, continued to occupy the tiny heads until, at last, the tin broke open. At first a *ting*, the sound of its opening then grew into the rasp of tearing metal, as the reek of pickling juice reached their nostrils, growing sharper as the tin was passed between Mohammad and Mounira. It was a process not so much of passing the

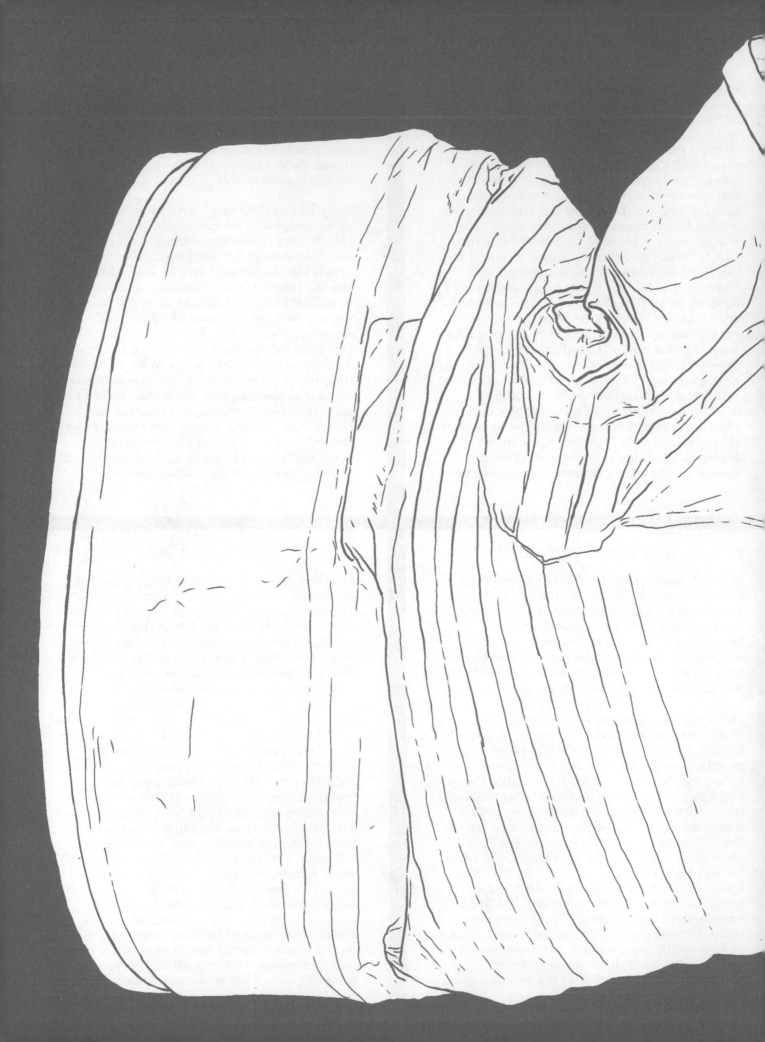

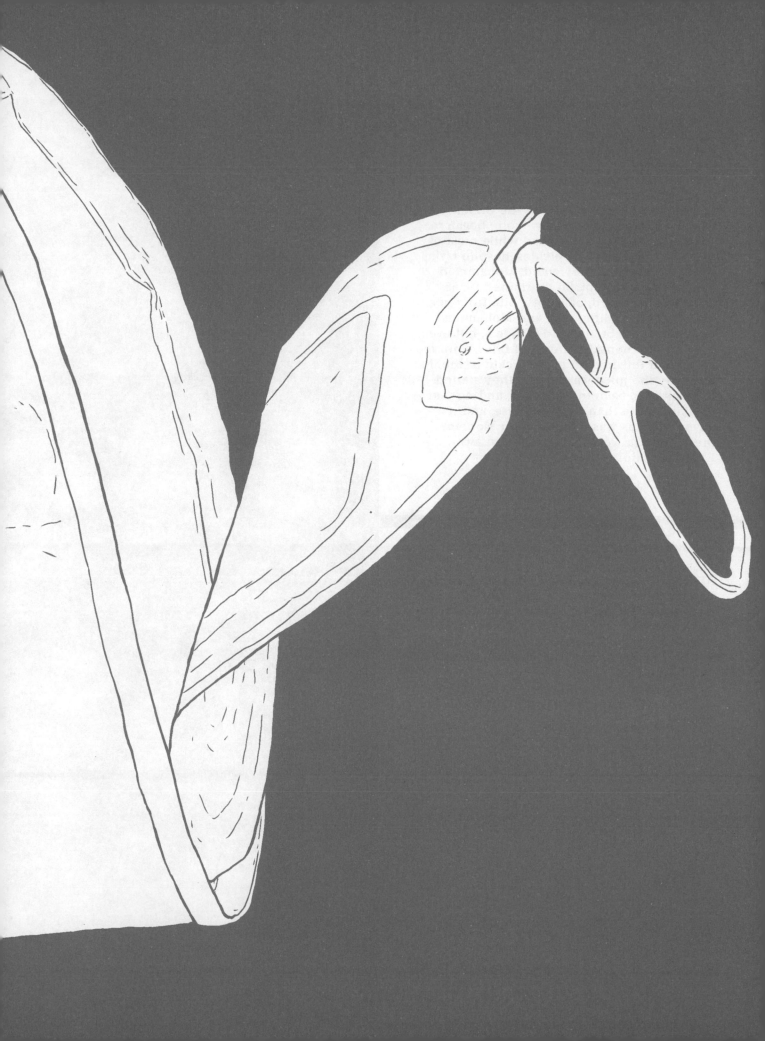

tin as of a reluctant parting, until it came
to rest at last in Mohammad's hands, while
Mounira went on taking out its contents.
Pickle by pickle, they were distributed first
to Maysoon, then to Mazen, then to Mukhles,
then to Moneim, and, finally, to Maya. And
truth be told, after much inspection and
examination, there didn't seem to be that
much difference in size. With Mohammad
and Mounira keeping hold of the tin and
whatever was left inside, everyone began to
gobble down their share. And while most of
them finished off their pickles, despite trying
to eat as slowly as they could, Mohammad
and Mounira did not. So murmured pleas
started to be heard, begging a bite from one or
the other, just a little one, and Mohammad
and Mounira rebuking the pleaders, but even
so, granting them the tiniest of bites, until the
group had finished off every pickle in the tin
and only the juice was left. So they started
to drink that, each in their turn, and no one
drinking more than everyone else, and if
anyone did, as was the case with Moneim,
then Mounira would snatch the tin away.
Fairly, we said!

Afterwards, Maya excluded, they split up into
two teams of three, and began punting the tin
back and forth between them. And whenever
the tin was kicked too far away, Maya, who
was standing on the side too young and too
small to know how to play football, would rush
to fetch it.

It was a truly beautiful day that none of
them would easily forget, ever. They were
happy.

THE HITTING BALL

In a society dependent on information and communication, a small sphere covered in characters allowed typefaces to grasp the zeitgeist or 'match the mood of your correspondence'.

Text by Paul Gangloff

In 1955, IBM workers John E. Hickerson, Ralph E. Page and James A. Weldenhammer came up with a device to which they first referred as the 'flying walnut', or 'bouncing ball'. It was a 'type element' designed to replace the type bars of a typewriter, in the form of a nine-gram sphere of plastic coated in nickel, from which the characters of the alphabet were protruding. Lower case and capital letters, numerals and punctuation signs were distributed around the small globe in four rows of twenty-two signs. Eventually nicked named 'golf ball', it is in fact, with a diameter of 32 mm, sensibly smaller than a golf ball, the diameter of which is about 42 mm. The characters on the ball are mirrored in order to leave a correct (inverted) mark on the paper when striking the ink ribbon. There is a madness in a spherical object designed to hit from all its sides at a speed of 14.8 strokes per second. Unlike most balls that are designed to be hit at (like an actual golf ball), this ball was the one doing the hitting. But the real power of the golf ball lies in its replaceability. One can remove it and insert a new one in the typewriter in 'just five seconds'.

In a society becoming increasingly dependent on information and communication, this technology made it possible, affordable and desirable to purchase typefaces, 'to match the mood of your correspondence' as an IBM advertisement put it. Typefaces named *Advocate*, *Orator*, *Delegate* or *Adjutant* were obviously designed for business and administration purposes. These are fonts made to convince, to bring an authority and a clarity, a sense of definiteness to the words typed with them. Other designs are more about distinguishing one's communications from others through style, as is the case of *Prestige Elite*, *Bookface Academic* or *Script*. Typefaces like *Courier* and *Letter Gothic* survived the obsolescence of the golf balls and are now available on almost every computer, used for film scripts, grey literature, or to remind the reader that someone has been typing the words he or she is reading.

The Selectric typewriter turned out to be a success; the market for golf balls grew. Not only did the many machines have to be equipped with several fonts, the balls also got worn out and had to be replaced

Press Roman
is a practical type
face featuring
excellent form and
clarity.
It is a sturdily
constructed face,
rich in feeling.

Press
IBM had initially contacted Stanley Morison, the designer of *Times New Roman*. Having refused to sign the non-disclosure agreement, he was driven straight back to the airport (he is quoted saying that if they didn't trust him, he didn't want to see anything). Apparently, IBM had counted on Morison's participation — they had been using *Times New Roman* to develop the Composer. IBM's approach to the copyright problem caused by Morison's refusal to sign the agreement and his subsequent departure, was to simply rename the *Times New Roman* on their golf balls *Press*.

Olde
English
Adds a look of
distinction
to special
announcements,
invitations,
greetings,

after a while. To answer the demand, a company named GP started to manufacture compatible type balls. With an extensive catalogue, it proposed a variety of typefaces from fraktur-looking (*Olde English*) to 'calligraphic' (*Calligraphy*), to designs attempting to grasp the zeitgeist (*Contempo*), next to imitations of the IBM fonts (*Courier, Prestige Elite, Orator*, etc.). GP introduced fun elements to its typefaces like the *Sunshine* feature available on a few golf balls, which allowed to type a smiley symbol by striking successively two keys, each of them typing a half of the smiling face. Such detailed typographic knowledge of the Selectric is to be found in the expanding *typosphere*, the community of bloggers who collect and use typewriters to 'typecast', publish on their blogs by means of photographed or scanned typescripts. A typecast on the blog *Claudia's Tappy Typewriters* reads: 'The final shipment of my IBM golfballs arrived today (...) This particular one was the most difficult to find. It boasts the ORIENTAL typeface (...) I had to laugh at the stereotype...' Indeed, the typeface was designed to fit the need to 'bring the intriguing flair of the orient' into 'menus, newsletters, gift cards'. Claudia's typecast gives an occasion to reflect on the problems of a culture that designs typography for such typification of an 'oriental other'.

GLOBALIZING THE GOLF BALL

The interchangeability of the golf balls also made the Selectric a truly *international* business machine. With a capacity of 88 characters, a ball could be equipped with accented letters and special characters. Balls were designed for each of thirteen different languages using the Latin alphabet. Non-Latin alphabetic writing systems were available as well: there were balls for Greek and for different languages using Cyrillic. Since the lateral movement of the ball across the paper could be reversed from left-to-right to right-to-left, it was even possible to run golf balls with Arabic, Hebrew and Farsi scripts. There were balls bearing phonetic alphabets like the Japanese Katakana or the Americanist phonetic notation, with which one could type a number of North American

Sunshine Script adds a special feature: two characters ☺ and ☻. Brings a happy face ☺ to your correspondence.

Monde
At the time the first sketches of what would become *Univers* were made, the typeface was called *Monde* (World). But the foundry's director, Charles Peignot, preferred a word that would have a more international sound.

Univers is a strong type face, *minus* typographical eccentricities.

indigenous languages. A Yiddish type ball was designed, 'equipped with all the letters, digraphs and diacritics needed to produce immaculate typescript in Yiddish in the standard or any other orthography'. And beyond writing systems for spoken languages was a type ball for Labanotation, the notation system for human movement, designed by choreographer Rudolf Laban in the 1920s. For further refinement, a golf ball could be customized. One could order additional characters to fit the needs of one's writing. Different currencies, technical, mathematical, chemical and medical symbols were available, as well as a miscellany of signs like arrows, a trade mark or a copyright sign.

The golf ball introduced typographic possibilities allowing businesses, administrations, institutions and individuals to type in the language they wanted to, without having to miss the signs that make it singular. In doing so, it also brought the Selectric typewriter onto more and more desks throughout the world. The success of the golf ball is to be considered within the context of the conquest of global communication by American technology. The great diversity of type balls goes together with the growing monopoly of companies like IBM in communication technologies across large parts of the world.

BEYOND MONOSPACE

Despite the variety of typefaces available as golf balls, all of them belong to the same category of typefaces: monospaced font. Typewriters, with or without golf balls, allocated the same space to each sign, letter, cipher, punctuation, proceeding one single unit at a time. In monospaced fonts each sign, from the thinnest, the *i* or the exclamation mark to the widest, the *w* or the *m,* occupies the same unit of space. This constraint is a great challenge to the creativity of type designers — in some cases resulting in beautiful designs, with quirky serifs extending the slim signs into their unit of space or extremely condensed letterforms — but it also makes the rhythm of the letters, words and sentences, the texture of the text, very monotonous, space consuming and unfit for longer texts.

IBM Selectric. From: *Your IBM Selectric Typewriter Manual*

IBM
SPECIAL FONT
IT MANIFESTS
SANS SERIF
1234567890=
*@#$%¢&½()

Motion
In advertising language, the motion of the type element was described as dancing on the paper. This formulation evacuates the typewriter's heritage as a descendant from a line of machines, the first generations of which rolled off the factories of Remington, a gun manufacturer. To promote the Selectric, a film was shot (yet another shooting technology), showing the action of the golf ball in slow motion. We see it through a macro lens as it revolves, tilts, strikes, moves laterally, revolves again, tilts again, strikes again.

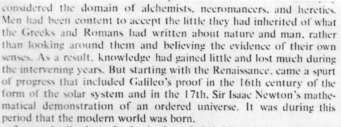

considered the domain of alchemists, necromancers, and heretics. Men had been content to accept the little they had inherited of what the Greeks and Romans had written about nature and man, rather than looking around them and believing the evidence of their own senses. As a result, knowledge had gained little and lost much during the intervening years. But starting with the Renaissance, came a spurt of progress that included Galileo's proof in the 16th century of the form of the solar system and in the 17th, Sir Isaac Newton's mathematical demonstration of an ordered universe. It was during this period that the modern world was born.

Leonardo lived at the beginning of this dynamic transition. His observations and experiments contributed much to its development

to believe that mathematics supplied a certain means of scientific proof and statement, thus anticipating the modern concept of mathematics as the language of science. For him mechanics was "the paradise of the mathematical sciences, because by means of it one comes to the fruits of mathematics." The many devices, whether practical or theoretical, that he sketched and described in his notebooks, and the models that have been made to illustrate a number of them, are demonstrations of this belief.

Where others saw only a bewildering diversity, Leonardo saw the

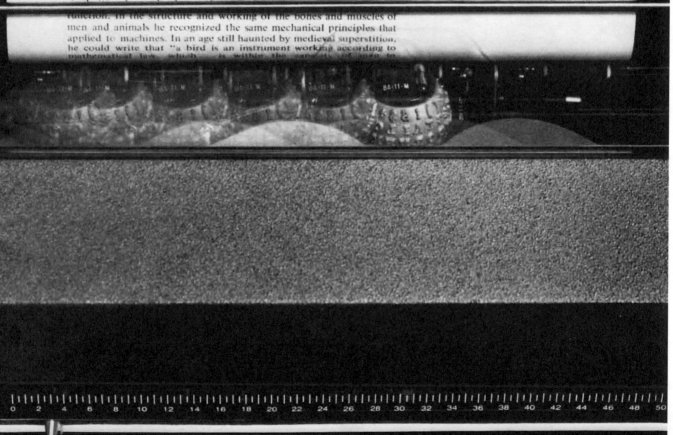

function. In the structure and working of the bones and muscles of men and animals he recognized the same mechanical principles that applied to machines. In an age still haunted by medieval superstition, he could write that "a bird is an instrument working according to mathematical law, which is within the capacity of man to

IBM Selectric. From: *IBM Composer Type Styles Portfolio*

IBM Selectric Golfballs. From: *IBM Composer Type Styles Portfolio*

The latest generation of golf balls was designed to overcome this. In 1964, having had the Swiss type designer Adrian Frutiger sign a non-disclosure agreement, IBM engineers introduced him to their new technology: the Selectric Composer. Frutiger called it 'a miracle' as he was presented the sample produced on this large typewriter: the text was typed in *Times New Roman*. What used to demand complex professional machinery that only large press corporations and professional printers could afford could now be done on this augmented typewriter.

Having developed the first typewriter-like machine to output proportional fonts, people at IBM probably wanted it to run the very best ones, which might be why they commissioned Frutiger to customize *Univers*, his elegant, rational sans serif typeface, for the golf ball. Freed from the restriction of the single-unit monospaced font, the Composer's golf ball was nevertheless ruled by another, more fine and flexible system of units that had been built upon the measurements of the characters of *Times New Roman*. To fit *Univers* on the golf ball, Frutiger had to force it into these units, encountering some tricky situations, from which, according to him, some rather unsatisfying solutions emerged. The *s* had to be drawn within four units instead of the five it needed. Same for the *g*, which is much narrower in a classic roman typeface than in a grotesque sans serif.

Eventually, the Selectric Composer would have a catalogue of more than fifteen different typefaces, with roman and italics in different cuts (Light, Regular, Medium, Bold) and different sizes (from 7 to 11 points), amounting to a total of 146 different balls available in the English catalogue. The quality of its typography and its relative affordability made the Selectric Composer instrumental for the independent publishing of the late 1960s and 1970s counterculture. It was a device much loved by the Californian pioneers of cybernetics who used it to typeset the emblematic and influential Whole Earth Catalog, a mail order catalogue offering 'access to tools' to a growing number of adepts of a culture at the crossings of ecology, technology and DIY hippie communes. In the last years of its career, the Selectric Composer would be

Whole Earth Catalog
The Selectric composer was crucial to the American counterculture magazine Whole Earth Catalog. As editor Stewart Brand wrote in his 1974 article *How to do a Whole Earth Catalog*: 'We publish considerable detailed information — fine print. Sorting among that is aided by a consistent code of type-faces (reviews are always "Univers italic", access is always "teeny", Divine Right is always "bold teeny", and so forth). The IBM Selectric Composer makes this an easy matter.' (sic)

A Super 8 film documenting the making of the 'Difficult But Possible Supplement' to the Catalog in the Californian desert, in 1971 is available online. It shows the editors of the Catalog with members of the avant-garde architecture collective Ant Farm setting up a dome-shaped inflatable hosting a couple of smaller geodesic domes and the editorial office/design studio. In its midst, a Selectric Composer's golf ball performed its revolutions.

Charles & Ray Eames, Eero Saarinen, *IBM World's Fair Pavillon*, New York, 1964–65

converted into a terminal for the first com-
puters, allowing to enter data and to print
it out. Then, a generation of electronic
typewriters appeared, in which the golf ball
was replaced by the faster 'daisy wheel'
a circular device having letter hammers at
the ending of plastic 'petals'.

PRECIOUS METAL

Since the mid-1980s typefaces are software,
but we still call them *fonts,* a word that
refers to the casting of letterforms from hot
metal as was done in type foundries. The
golf ball relied on a typographic printing
technique five hundred years old and yet
its behaviour in relation to the typewriter
already announced the software/hardware
paradigm. It was still a kind of moveable
type and yet also already desktop publishing technology.
    The golf ball has probably been the last
material format of typefaces, after which
it has been deemed more advantageous to
have all type as software stored on different
memories. It is almost bizarre to think that
not so long ago one could drop the typeface

on the floor, and pick it up. Now that it is
relegated to the category of obsolete technology, the golf ball has gained a new power
of attraction on collectors. It might draw this
power from a longing for materiality that we
develop, as the technology we use for our
communication is becoming ungraspable.
Or is it because it descends from a lineage
of objects the first of which were made
by Johannes Gutenberg, a 15th-century
goldsmith?

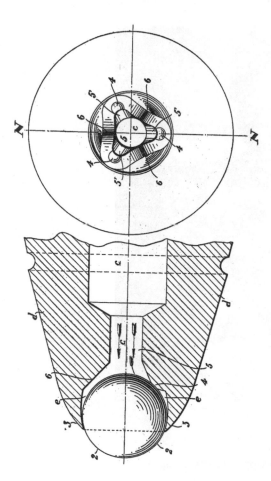

László Bíró, Ballpoint Pen Patent, 1943

BALL

POINT

Through a combination of stubbornness and obsessiveness, László Bíró invented everything from an automatic gearbox to a cigarette filter, but he is best remembered as the inventor of the ballpoint pen, which changed the way we write.

Text by Merel Boers

László Bíró, c. 1960. Photo Paul Popper/Getty Images

Ballpoint, biro, Kugelschreiber, BIC... The history of the ball-tipped pen is surprisingly torturous. It is a story that does not revolve around the ball, but around the ink. It took a single-minded inventor, a man who readily sacrificed money, family, friends and business partners, to make a ballpoint pen that worked.

From the end of the 19th century, a number of inventors had tried to patent and produce a ballpoint pen, and failed each time. As a writing tool that was supposed to replace leaky fountain pens, it was all too leaky itself. And the ink dried up too quickly in the reservoir, just as it did in fountain pens. The pen we use today was invented by the Hungarian László Bíró, and first produced in 1943. Which is why Brits still know a biro when they see one.

Bíró was an inventor as one imagines them. A restless man, always working on new ideas, always moving from job to job, from place to place, often leaving his family behind. A man with a flair for creating his own myth, and incredibly stubborn. It is this stubbornness that eventually won the day for the ballpoint. Because the investors he visited with his prototypes were not really interested in a new ballpoint pen: they had seen them before, and they never worked. They still had plenty of 'Mungo' pens lying around, a defective German ballpoint introduced in 1924.

Bíró had invented an automatic gearbox; General Motors bought it from him, to make sure it would not reach the market. Being tricked like this left him angry, but the money gave him room for his main obsession: his ballpoint pen. When money was tight, he would sit in his favourite hangout, a coffee house in Budapest called the Japan Café, bumming coffee-and-milk refills from sympathetic waiters. With his stubborn belief in himself, he managed to scrape together more money and supporters every time things got tight. Then he went back to his rooms, where the walls were ink-stained from explosive pen-experiments. (In the meantime, his wife took on different jobs to support herself and their daughter.)

Stubborn Bíró recruited a small band of faithfuls who helped him turn his idea into a working product. That was no small feat, considering all of the leaky, scratchy, dried-up ballpoint pens that came before. There was his brother György, a dentist, who (in Bíró's version of the story) did not have his brother's soaring imagination, but a precise hand for menial laboratory work, meaning: testing the ink. There was his friend Imre Gellért, who supported him financially in the early days. There was the Hussar György Meyne, a flamboyant creature good with people (especially women) and advertising campaigns. And, most importantly, there was Andor Goy. Goy was an inventor in his own right: he had invented a typewriter with an automatic carriage. Later in life he developed a typesetting machine, the Typopress. A highly disciplined, self-made man, Goy was the one who paid for the patent of the pens and the ink cartridge, in the spring of 1938. Goy then took to the road to find a manufacturer, in a Europe on the cusp of war. Meanwhile, Bíró continued his inksperiments, for which Goy had given him an advance.

The Bíró band left a trail of dye-paste wherever they went, staining and splattering hotel rooms and potential business partners. But the times did not favour them. Bíró was Jewish, and the Hungarian Nazi party, the Arrow Cross, was on the rise. All around him, Jewish friends and colleagues were leaving. The last time he spoke to Goy was on 23 December 1938: they wrote up a new contract with regard to patent, distribution and the division of profits. Bíró left Budapest on New Year's Day. He was on the move, like so many European Jews at the time. Eventually he reached Buenos Aires, by way of Paris and Barcelona. In the fall of 1941, his family joined him.

In Argentina, Bíró was sponsored by a Hungarian couple, the Lángs, who had also helped him emigrate. An affidavit was drawn up, wherein Bíró one-sidedly detached himself from his European business partners — first among them Goy. The Lángs then set up a company intended to profit from patent royalties once the pen had been developed. (They would later relieve Bíró of all his shares in the company.) With the help of some other bigger investors — Meyne reeled in the Dutch company

The Bíró band left a trail of dye-paste wherever they went

Philips — Bíró set up a little factory cum laboratory.

Work on the ink problem continued full force. The ink needed to stay fluid in the pen, but dry quickly on paper. It should not clog around the ball-tip. The writing flow should be uninterrupted. The solution was to move from a water-based ink (as in fountain pens) to an oil-based dye paste. Even then, the Bíró brothers tinkered with the formula for years, to get the proportions just right. The secret ingredient was never revealed by Bíró (it was glycol).

The ink was not the only technical challenge that the ballpoint pen provided. Earlier, Goy had improved the ink flow by making the hole bigger with a triangular file, and thus discovered that three tiny notches in the ball socket made for a more regular distribution of ink on the paper. In Argentina, Bíró found out the hard way that the 1 mm metal ball needed to be perfectly spherical — elliptical balls made for an interrupted flow. One eureka moment was born from fatigue, when he forgot to place back the plunger after filling the ink-cartridge, and found the pen worked better when it was open, without the plunger to push the ink down.

By 1943, the ballpoint pen was finally working well enough to conquer the world. It did not only take a lot of ink, but also a little bluff to bring the Biro pen to market. Here Meyne came in handy again. He engineered an enormous marketing campaign for which he intended to pay only much later, when the money had started rolling in. He even included a bit of fake news: that an eventual peace treaty would be signed with their pen. Bíró honoured Meyne's efforts by naming the pen after them both: Birome. The rest, as they say, is history.

Yet both Bíró and Goy ended up empty-handed. Through a combination of naïveté, honour and stubbornness, both lost the rights to their life's work. Goy had tried to get the dye-paste formula from Bíró, which he thought a fair honouring of their pre-war agreement; Bíró denied his request. Using another dye, Goy then tried to develop his own pen, the Gopen; but soon the Hungarian state nationalized his factory and most of his private property. He had not seen it coming. In the 1950s, he was involved in a joint West-German-Hungarian lawsuit, an effort to get a slice of the patent. It failed. Goy had a chance to move to West Germany, but in the end he chose to stay in Hungary.

Meanwhile, Bíró had managed to sign over all his shares and thus missed out on the roaring success of his hard work. A lot of money was being made with the ballpoint pen: other manufacturers (Reynolds, BIC) paid steep royalties. But not to Bíró or Goy. They ended their lives at odds with one another: Bíró angry about the lawsuit; Goy never forgiving Bíró for breaking their contract.

Bíró survived by the wits of his wife Elza, who had always managed to make and save some money of her own (and keep him from investing it). He never stopped inventing. A heavy smoker, he made a cigarette filter; a wristband that measured one's pulse. For various reasons, these inventions did not take flight — although the cigarette filter was much appreciated by president Perón. He went bankrupt on a perfume roller that worked on the same principle as

Aber die Kugel, die rollt

the ballpoint. 'Only fools are interested in successes,' Bíró told a Hungarian interviewer in the 1970s. 'Anyone who has taken a creative process from start to finish will know from first hand how little it would have taken for it to have failed along the way.'

As Goy once wrote: *aber die Kugel, die rollt.*

Source: György Moldova, *Ballpoint: A Tale of Genius and Grit, Perilous Times, and the Invention That Changed the Way We Write* (2012)

A VERY BIC SUCCESS

Bíró's pen was the first to really work, but the most famous ballpoint is produced by BIC, the company of French Baron Marcel Bich. In the late 1940s Bich, who later dropped the 'h' to become the easy-to-remember BIC (and according to some, to avoid the association with 'bitch'), designed his own disposable, mass-produced, cheap ballpoint. He approached the Bíró brothers and arranged to pay them a royalty on their patent. Bich then took two years to develop a viscosity of ink that had to prevent leaking, and, in December 1950, launched a clear-barrelled, six-sided ballpoint that would become

a design classic: the *BIC Cristal*, followed by an equally successful retractable model. The hexagonal transparent barrel of the *Cristal* was a modern take on the wooden pencil, showing the level of ink and allowing it to flow into the point with the help of a tiny hole that maintained the same air pressure inside and outside the pen. Bich invested heavily in advertising, hiring famous poster designer Raymond Savignac in 1952 to design the first, prize-winning BIC advertising campaign 'Elle court, elle court la pointe Bic'. Ten years later, Savignac created the iconic BIC logo of a schoolboy with a shiny ballpoint head. Consequently, the *BIC Cristal* conquered the market and the (art) world. In 1965 the French government approved its use in schools, with other countries following suit. Artists like Andy Warhol and Alighiero Boetti used BIC pens as a medium to express the merging of high and low culture (see inside back cover).

In the 1970 decade of disposables, BIC expanded its line to include throwaway felt-tip pens,

razors and cigarette lighters. The BIC Crystal remains the flagship though; with an estimated worldwide 15 million BIC ballpoints sold every day, predictions that the writing was on the wall for pens in the digital age seem as premature as the dream of a paperless office.

KA

Left: Baron Marcel Bich, c. 1950
Above: BIC Crystal, 1950. Courtesy BIC Group

2.
TO SHINE

A mirrored moon, an astrological tool, a feel-good figure, a psycho killer... Balls are in abundance in Part 2 as we deconstruct the disco, spread some smileys, play with marbles and predict the future.

81 ✳ ✳ ✳ ✳ ✳ ✳ ✳ ✳
✳ ✳ ✳ ✳ ✳ DISCO
✳ ✳ ✳ ✳
BALL
✳
OF ✳ ✳
✳ ✳ DESIRE ✳ ✳

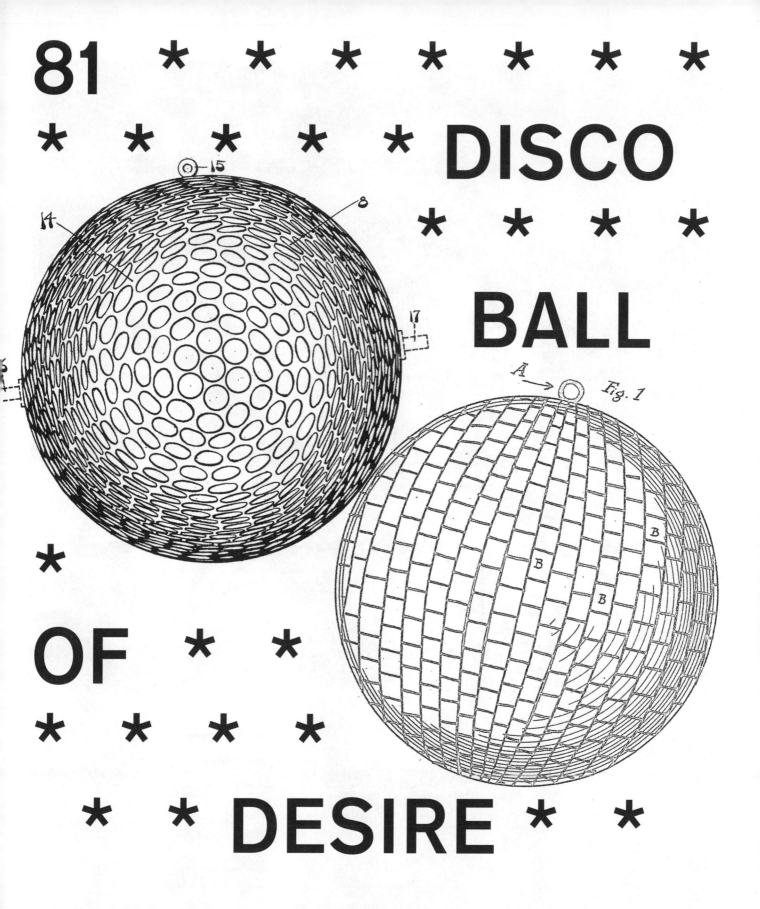

Under a fairy sky where a mirrored moon dances with an artificial sun, the disco floor seethes with the rituals of rhythms and desiring gazes.

Text by Pol Esteve

Le Jardin Disco, New York, 1970s. Photo Allan Tannenbaum

Since the invention of the oil lamp, lighting systems have transformed the spaces we inhabit and altered our conception of the world. Scientific advances from the 18th century onwards have given us increasingly brighter and cheaper technologies for lighting, making rational clarity ubiquitous. The rapid spread of artificial light physically manifested a wider cultural enterprise. The Enlightenment made light not only a powerful metaphor within western culture, but also a project for inhabited space.

By the 19th century, electric light started to colonize all spaces of the western world, making cities visible from beyond the stratosphere. Private and public spaces were flooded in light. In homes, as well as in spaces of production and consumption, factories and shopping malls, activity could continue without interruption under artificial lighting. Streetlamps permanently illuminated the city and flickering traffic lights regulated its flows. The daily cycle of brightness and darkness was interrupted by the possibility of everlasting light. Breaking the astrological rhythm of light became a sign of modernity and technological optimism.

In the 20th century, however, a new and ambiguous object subverted the aim of propagating clarity: the mirror ball, otherwise known as the disco ball. This is a spherical object of variable size covered by hundreds of tiny mirrors. It normally hangs from a mechanical system, which makes it rotate, attached to the ceiling of a room. An artificial light source shines onto the mirrors, which shatter the light and reflect hundreds of rays in all directions, which in turn cast a myriad of bright spots onto the surrounding surfaces.

Some accounts trace the history of the disco ball to the early 20th century. The first patent for an object similar to a disco ball was issued in the United States in 1917 to Louis Bernard Woeste, for his 'Myriad Reflector'. In 1929, Woeste received a second patent for an object with the same name. His entry included a more detailed drawing of the object. Both entries present a spherical object covered in small mirrors. The first shows rectangular mirrors, the second circular mirrors held by folded metal clips. Neither of the two included a

Myriad reflector in the parlour of a sanatorium in Milwaukee, 1912. Courtesy Wisconsin Historical Society

rotating mechanism. Other histories trace the presence of mirror-covered globes in ballrooms and jazz clubs in the early decades of the 20th century. A picture held in the archive of the Wisconsin Historical Society also shows a mirrored ball hanging from the ceiling in the parlour of a sanatorium in Milwaukee. Press reviews and product catalogues from the period presented the mirror ball as a technical novelty capable of projecting fairy lights like stars.

After its first appearance, the mirror ball languished for a long time. It wasn't until the late 1960s, as disco music gained popularity, that it became an indispensable element in the discotheque and a defining symbol of an era. The image of the disco ball immediately calls to mind all sorts of crowded dance floors associated with disco, house and other genres of music. It instantly evokes a spatial experience augmented by psychotropic substances, electronically produced music, and all sorts of lighting effects. Along with subwoofers, ultraviolet lights, flashing lights and laser lights, it creates an architecture of intense sensory experience. Yet the significance of the disco ball extends much further. The mirrored sphere stands for the social and political transformations triggered and rendered visible by the ritual of dancing.

The early 1970s are widely regarded as the peak of an intellectual crisis that ushered in postmodernity. After a gradual process of decadence, philosophical precepts that edified the modern world were finally contested. The role of the body and perception were reconsidered at all levels, from the intellectual sphere to the world of pop culture. It was a time when thinkers theoretically articulated alternatives to the established perceptual order. The intellectual historian Martin Jay recounts in his book *Downcast Eyes: The Denigration of Vision in Twentieth-Century French Thought* how in the 1970s French intellectuals dismantled the perceptual regime that dominated modern times, which he calls 'phallogocularcentrism'. Jay uses this neologism, 'phallogocularcentrism', to denote a system dominated by masculine vision over other senses and subjectivities. With the impulse of new feminism, theoretical voices challenged such gender imbalance and sensory reduction, claiming the full body as an instrument of emancipation.

    With regard to the material world, the essential tool in constructing the scopic regime of phallogocularcentrism is light: the retina needs an illuminated medium to see. That is why the ancient metaphor of the sun, already present in Plato's myth of the cave and at the root of western culture, was central to enlightenment. Light was the vehicle that allowed the masculine subject to understand the physical world and dominate the realm of ideas. As Foucault pointed out, modernity made of vision an instrument of truth, while obscurity and blindness were considered its threatening opposite. In the absence of natural light, artificial light would bring clarity to the eye. With the replacement of the sun by the lamp, clarity became disposable. In spaces like the operating theatre, the police interrogation room and the street, artificial clarity revealed and regulated the abnormal. Such was the power and symbolic value of artificial light that, even during French revolution, street lamps were destroyed because they were symbols

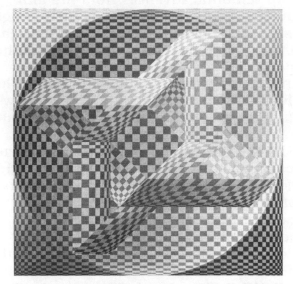

Ben Cunningham, *Equivocation*, 1964. MoMA, *The Responsive Eye*, 1965, catalogue

of control. In the 19th century, with the spread of electricity, intellectuals stood up and reclaimed the twilight, without much success.

Prominent deconstructivist and feminist thinkers of the 1970s, among them Derrida and Irigaray, opened the door and broke up the dichotomy between light and dark, the visible and the invisible, established under the phallogocularcentric regime. Rather than merely negating such a binary system, they found emancipation by exalting it. As Jay recalls, in the dazzling overload of the perceptual system created by op art, some people saw a theoretical search aimed at dissolving the central role of the eye. In 1965, the seminal op art exhibition held at the MoMA under the title *The Responsive Eye* featured a series of geometric and colourful compositions that overloaded the eye with striking and illusionary visual effects. 'What are the potentialities of a visual art capable of affecting perception so physically and directly?,' William C. Seitz asks in the catalogue. 'Can an advanced application of functional images open a new path from retinal excitation to emotions and ideas?'

And what is the disco ball if not an expanded form of op art? The works of Victor Vasarely, Joël Stein and Yaacov Agam shown in the exhibition are almost static representations of the mirror ball. Multiple circular and elliptical shapes in different tones and intensities emulate movement and change as if they photographically captured spots of light cast by disco balls. If there is a difference between the gallery and the dance floor, it is that the spectacle on the dance floor happens among the public, not in front of it. In film, another art form made with light, the body of the spectator is left out and does not participate directly in the action. Cinema, however, was already seen as a space that embeds the gaze with desire and offers alternatives to the masculine perspective. Visual overstimulation and desiring gazes are constituent elements of the dance floor experience, yet there is a difference with the gallery and cinema: the disco ball breaks open permanent vision. Playfully intertwining vision and blindness, the revolving and flashing lights only find expression in the darkness.

The postmodern critique of the phenomenological approach to perception denounced the lack of consideration of instability and discontinuation in a phenomenological approach to perception, as exemplified by the blink of the eye. As Jay writes: 'The eye that knows when to blink or shut is thus preferable to the one that stares without eyelids in the full glare of the light of reason, but such an eye still at times knows when to look.' The disco ball both conceals and reveals, makes you blink and stare. The rays of light expose with precision highlighted fragments of the surroundings. Like chronphotography, it instantly freezes forms on the retina. The surrounding darkness hides the rest. Like film, it leaves part of the actions out of the frame in order to maintain the illusion. The alternating transition from seen to unseen casts a spell on the senses. Under the spell of the disco ball, the dancer's body assumes an indefinite position. He becomes blind and sighted, the object of the gaze and the subject who sees.

From an architectural perspective, the disco ball appears to be the ultimate postmodern instrument. In a deconstructive ritual, it collapses vision and breaks apart the hierarchy of the senses. As a consequence of the overstimulation of the eye, the focus shifts to the body and its temporal rhythms — a shift, praised by feminists, against the sterile spatialization of the eye. Yet the moving body creates its own space. In *The Architecture of Deconstruction*, Anthony Vidler writes that 'the deconstructive dance is not a particular kind of movement through an already constituted space, but is itself a spacing that at once subverts and produces space'. His words involuntarily describe the effects of the disco ball: triggering the retina to subvert visual space and propelling the body to dance and produce space by gesturing and interacting with other bodies, sound and lights.

With a seemingly simple game of reflections, the disco ball represents and activates a space that materializes the theoretical displacements of postmodern thought. From phallogocularcentrism to the hyper-visual, from one-way perception to the reciprocal desiring gaze, from the eye to the full body. Not surprisingly, some of the most famous disco balls were found in queer dance clubs like the Warehouse in Chicago and the Continental Baths and the Paradise Garage in New York. The assertion of gender, racial and sexual differences, which emerged around the same time and put the focus on the body as a container of political and social struggles, could not have found expression but under a fairy sky where a mirrored moon was dancing with an artificial sun.

Crisco Disco, New York, 1979. Photo Bill Bernstein

David Manusco's The Loft, New York, 1982. Courtesy Louis 'Loose' Kee Jr.

FROM BASEMENT TO WAREHOUSE

The return of the mirror ball in the 1970s was linked to the emergence of disco music. Having developed out of soul and R&B, disco found an audience in Black, Latino, Italian and gay communities on the east coast of United States, particularly in New York, from the late 1960s. Disco was initially played in nightclubs that also offered live music and were mostly frequented by members of those communities.

Not surprisingly, one of the first disco venues was a gay sauna. *Continental Baths* opened in 1968 in the basement of the Ansonia Hotel, located at 230 West 74th Street in New York. The club boasted not only a disco and cabaret lounge, but also

baths, cabins and a swimming pool. In the early 1970s, artists like Bette Midler launched their careers on the stage at the Continental. Over the years the space was reconfigured to incorporate an advanced sound system and psychedelic lighting effects. The 1975 film *Saturday Night in the Baths* features the club interior, complete with disco ball and high-energy lighting. That same year, a *Continental Baths* ad in a local gay guide touted the venue as the world's only 24-hour discotheque.

Continental Baths would close that same year, yet many other New York discotheques acquired legendary status, among them *The Loft* (opened in 1970) and *Paradise Garage* (opened in 1977). David Mancuso launched his 'Loft' parties at his own home but

relocated in 1975 to a venue in Soho, which became a disco. The quality of the sound system at *Paradise Garage* was such that resident DJ Larry Levan was said to make soundwaves resonate in the body cavities of dancers. *Studio 54*, the most famous disco of all, opened in 1977, but the list of revered dance clubs in the city was long, boasting such names as *Crisco Disco*, *Limelight* and *Starship Discovery*.

By the dawn of the 1980s, disco music began to inspire new genres of music, among them house. One of its pioneers was Frankie Knuckles, a DJ who started his career at the *Continental Baths*. He moved to Chicago in 1977 to become resident DJ at *The Warehouse*. Hence the name 'house music'.

Paradise Garage, New York, 1981. Photo DJ Bernie Bernthaler. Opposite page: *Disco Bats*, GG's Barnum Room, New York, 1979. Photo Bill Bernstein

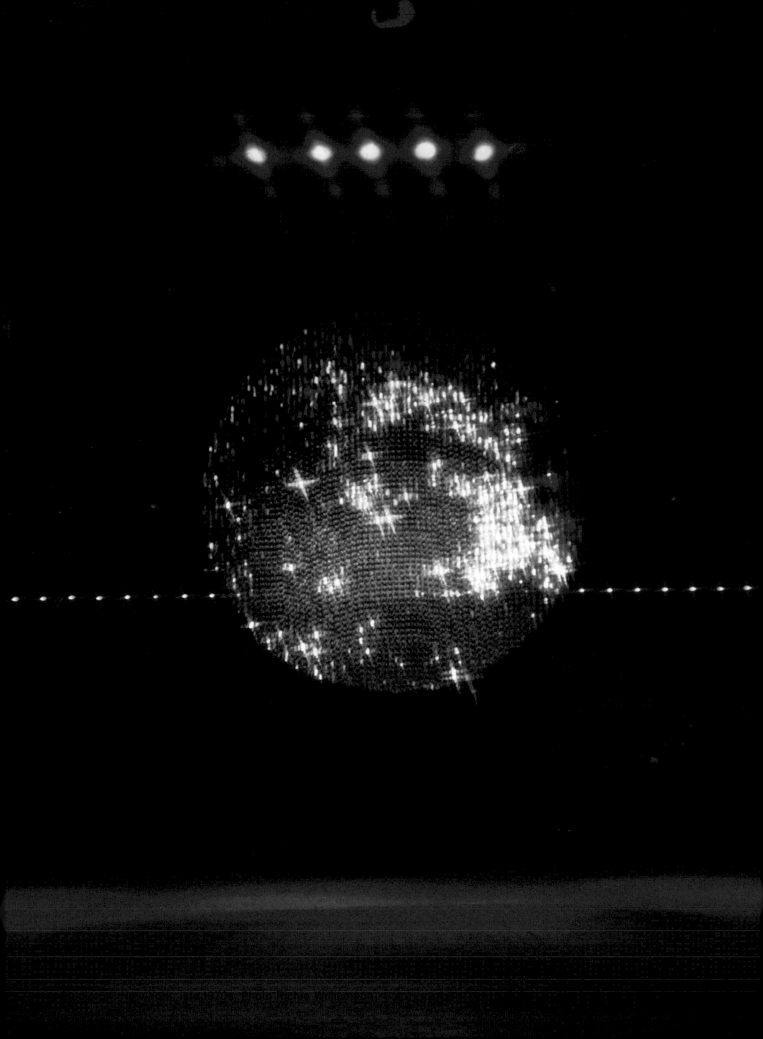

HARVEY BALL

The smiley earns 130 million US dollars a year in copyright fees, but the man who invented it earned a lousy 45 dollars for his work, a twist of fate that hasn't stopped him smiling.

Text by Lilian Stolk

Prehistoric objects have been found that show, whether by accident or by design, a smiling face, and there are letters written in the Middle Ages that end with one. But the iconic image of the yellow smiling ball has been attributed to the appropriately named American designer Harvey Ball. It is the grandfather of all modern emojis: the smiley.

Back before the Second World War, Ball learnt to make 'images with impact' from a local sign painter with whom he served an apprenticeship. It stood him in good stead later as a graphic designer. In 1963 he was commissioned by State Mutual Life Assurance to come up with an image for a 'friendship campaign'. A merger with another company had taken the atmosphere among employees to an all-time low. To drive out the resulting bitterness, the director of the insurance company asked Ball to design 'a smile' that could be printed on buttons, cards and posters.

It was a minor task that Ball tackled with great attention to detail. When he drew a semicircle on paper with a black felt pen, he was not immediately satisfied. More was needed. He drew two eyes above it and a circle around it, so that it became an actual face. He deliberately drew everything by hand, just short of perfection. One eye was slightly bigger than the other. Ball later said, 'I had a choice. Do I use a compass to draw the smiley and two perfect dots for the eyes? Nah, do it freely. Give it some character.' Within ten minutes the smiley was down on paper. It earned Ball $45.

The insurance company ordered a hundred buttons to remind staff to smile more often, both to each other and to their clients. The company hoped it might sell more insurance that way. Fairly soon it became clear that those hundred buttons were the start of something far bigger. Within a few years a hundred thousand buttons had been given away. Bernard and Murray Spain, two brothers from Philadelphia who ran a Hallmark shop, spotted how popular they were and saw the earnings potential. Without claiming copyright of the symbol, they decided to sell smiley buttons, coffee mugs, stickers and earrings in their shop, complete with the message 'Have a happy day'. Ball was delighted with the success, but neglected to apply for the copyright on his design. French journalist Franklin Loufrani beat him to

Illustrations by Harvey Ball for The Smiley Face Song (Ballad of Harvey Ball), written by his son Charlie Ball, 1998

it in 1971, by which time more than fifty million smiley buttons had been sold. Loufrani wanted to use the smiley in the newspaper he worked for, *France-Soir*, to highlight good news stories. He registered the design at the French patent office and now, with his son Nicolas Loufrani, he is the owner of the brand licensing firm The Smiley Company, which holds the rights to smiley face symbols in more than a hundred countries (excluding the US) and has an annual turnover of $130 million.

Ball has seen his smiley pop up everywhere. When the hippie era dawned in America in the 1960s, the smiley was the perfect feel-good symbol for propagating new ideas about love and freedom. But when in the mid-1970s shops were deluged with a myriad of smiley trinkets, the symbol began to become alienated from the counterculture. It now represented a society that was shutting its eyes to the horrors of the Vietnam War and the failures of the president. The happy face became frayed at the edges. American band Talking Heads used a smiley as an ironic image for the record sleeve of its number Psycho Killer, about the inner thoughts of a serial murderer. In the popular comic series Watchmen (1986), about a group of retired superheroes, a smiley button with a splash of blood adorns the main character's black outfit. The icon stands for society and the blood for its problems; in the comic the superheroes are given a dose of reality and heroic deeds are conspicuously absent. In the late 1980s, British DJ Danny

Rampling decided that the gloominess of youth culture must end. In Ibiza he was inspired to set up a new, eclectic nightclub in London, and in the smiley he discovered precisely what a night out should be: positivity wearing a big smile (with or without the help of Ecstasy). Rampling was responsible for turning the smiley into a symbol of acid house, and suddenly the yellow face once again became associated with pleasure and a free spirit.

Ball's smiley has become one of the most commonly used symbols on earth. Since 2011 its digital variant, the emoji, has been a feature of our smartphones. Six billion emojis are sent every day. Although others filled their own pockets with money from his design, Ball himself used the smiley above all in his charitable efforts. His World Smile Foundation licenses the use of the smiley in America, but all the proceeds go to a good cause, a charity that supports children facing problems. Ball was proud of having designed something with such widespread appeal that truly binds people together. Asked whether he had ever regretted not registering the copyright in a design that had such an impact, his standard answer was, 'Hey, I can only eat one steak at a time.'

ALL THE MARBLES

Scheltens & Abbenes revisited their childhood and discovered that marbles are still prized possessions. Pictured on these pages is a battered selection of their son's latest triumphs: the Giant, Hogger, Bumbo, Bonker, Bumboozer, Smasher, Masher, Popper, Plumper and Thumper.

Photography by Scheltens & Abbenes

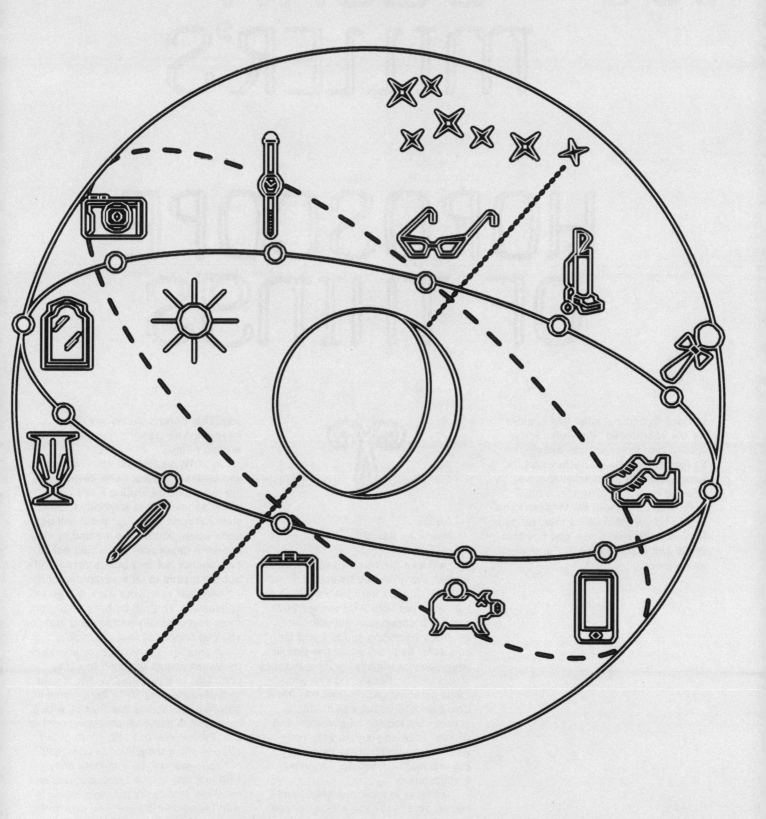

SUSAN MILLER'S

HOROSCOPE OF THINGS

Curious to find out what lies in store for the year ahead, MacGuffin knew who to turn to for advice: astrologist Susan Miller. She gladly forecast the future and told us exactly what we need to lead a fulfilling life: a high-tech vacuum cleaner for Virgo to keep things tidy, a Mont Blanc fountain pen for Pisces to sign those all-important deals and thank you notes, and much, much more.

1   ARIES
Mar. 20 – Apr. 20

You will love the coming year because Jupiter, the giver of gifts and luck, will be in Sagittarius from the very start of the New Year until 2 December 2019, and will broaden your outlook considerably by asking you to travel far and wide. Sagittarius is a fire sign like yours, so you will absorb the goodness of Jupiter effortlessly and see enormous personal growth from this trend. If you want to go back to graduate school, this too will be possible, and you will excel in your studies. You will now view projects in their largest and most successful panoramic manifestation.

Jupiter is in your intellectual ninth house, so all year you will be coaxed to learn, grow and to share the knowledge that you gain. The ninth house is closely associated with international travel, for travel is one of the very best ways to learn about the world around

you. This trend includes working internationally as well, possibly without leaving home.

In 2019, Jupiter will encourage you to design at least one awe-inspiring adventure by visiting a city or a paradise island that will likely require your passport for entry, and it will be somewhere you always wanted to visit but were never sure you would get to see. Jupiter not only brings opportunity but the means to take advantage of it.

Like last year, your work will be all consuming. You will be busy taking on more responsibility and proving that you can handle all that you tackle.

A prestigious new title, or an industry award seems destined to come your way. In your personal life, if your birthday falls near 15-19 April, you will surprise your family and friends with a courageous personal announcement in the first months of 2019, if you didn't already make a decision in late 2018.

Your year will be a thrilling one, with learning, career success, and an increase in industry prestige, along with breathtaking travel and growth in your personal love and family life, too. It's a year to remember — you will be making the news in your family.

Your 2019 MacGuffin: A beautiful, durable suitcase.

Text by Susan Miller
Drawings by Rosie Eveleigh

2 TAURUS
Apr. 21 – May 20

You are entering a very exciting period in your life, for Uranus, the planet of disruption, creativity, and sudden change will enter Taurus on 5 March and remain until 2026. Uranus takes 84 years to circle the Sun, so you will never have Uranus visit Taurus again. Remarkably, with Uranus in Taurus, your appearance may change, and you may even change your name. In your work, Uranus can make you quite famous, so if being well known is a dream of yours, over the coming seven years it appears that goal is there for the taking.

Uranus is the natural ruler of your career (tenth house), so you may start to shift the direction of your career. Uranus rules electricity, so you are likely to move closer to the digital world. Alternatively, you may develop more of an interest in politics, or humanitarian projects, for Uranus governs those areas too.

Jupiter, the giver of gifts and luck, has recently begun to move through your eighth house of other people's money. This should be a banner year for financial gain. If you are in sales, you may make impressive commissions, or if you write, a lucrative book advance and royalty package may come your way. If you earn your compensation on a performance basis you will be on the road to wealth. If you work for others, you can now negotiate fine company benefits.

If you need funds to fulfil a dream, 2019 is the year to apply, for your banker, student loan officer, or a certain venture capitalist will likely approve the money you need to get started.

Finally, love will be best when Mars, the passionate planet, moves through your true love sector, 17 August to 3 October. At the same time, Venus, the goddess of love, will also tour your true love sector from 21 August to 14 September. Venus and Mars are considered a glamorous pair and capable of setting off exciting fireworks for new love or for re-energizing the love for someone you have been

with, and love to this day. Single or attached, you are about to have fun.

Your 2019 MacGuffin: A piggy bank to remind you to save some of the large amounts of cash coming to you in 2019.

3 GEMINI
May 21 – June 20

Last year you focused on your health and fitness, and now, as you move into 2019, working in collaboration with experts will bring your greatest personal growth, and at work, profits too. Jupiter, the planet of good fortune, moved into your seventh house of partnership in late 2018 and is now ready to bring you rewards.

Your seventh house is essentially the place you negotiate serious contractual agreements of all kinds — including marriage. We generally don't think of marriage as a contract agreement, but it is the reason marriage is covered by the seventh house. Jupiter will remain in this area of your chart until 2 December 2019. If you marry before year's end, you will have chosen the very best year in 12 years to tie the knot. If you are already wed, you will see your partner prosper and you will benefit too through your partner's good fortune.

If you work in a field where others represent you, such as an agent, manager, lawyer or other collaborator, you can hire an expert to work with you who will work out to be a gem. Similarly, if you are an agent or work one-on-one with talent or clients, you will find one among them to be a star, and together you can go far. In 2019, collaboration will be your key to success.

In matters of love, October 2019 is likely to be your best month. Mars will circulate in your true love sector from 3 October to 18 November, suggesting you can start a new cycle in matters of the heart or add passion to a present, long-term relationship. Venus, the love-me planet, and your ruler, Mercury, will be in your love sector too, a good sign you'll be ready to give your heart to the one you love. If a relationship is new, enter into it slowly and enjoy it — there will be no need to rush.

Get engaged or wed after the 28 September new moon arrives, but avoid signing a prenuptial agreement together. Already wed? Save up for a fun activity that you can do together.

Your 2019 MacGuffin: A new smart phone with plenty of battery power to keep in touch with your partner in love or business in 2019.

4 CANCER
June 21 – July 22

The past seven years seems to have brought more than your share of career ups and downs due to changing conditions in your industry and company. You were hosting Uranus, the planet of unpredictability, sudden change, and disruption in your tenth house of prestigious career progress.

You may have changed jobs after a long loyalty to one particular company, shifted to a completely new industry, or opened your own business, and this was likely to have happened between 2011 and 2018. You knew you were most suited to a job that gave you a large measure of autonomy and freedom without being overly supervised and you searched for that kind of circumstance.

Jupiter quietly moved into Sagittarius in late 2018, to stay until 2 December 2019. By the start of 2019, he will be ready to help you from your sixth house of work-a-day projects, so your work life is about to become much more interesting and busy. You will not have to look far to generate more business or to be given plum assignments. Under Jupiter in Sagittarius, your workplace may be upgraded with software, hardware, and your surroundings may become more comfortable.

Also, with Jupiter in Sagittarius, you will have the best year in over a decade to get fit and strong. If you need to seek advice for a medical concern that requires special treatment or surgery, with research you are likely to discover a doctor who understands your condition and whom you trust. Attend to that medical concern in advance of 2 December 2019.

If you are single and you started dating someone special in 2018, that person may be someone right for a long-term relationship, very possibly for forever. If you did not meet anyone, the new moon, 4 November 2019, may bring opportunity in the days to follow. If you are attached, you, too, will enjoy more attention from your partner after that new moon.

Additionally, when Mars enters Scorpio, he will energize your fifth house love sector, to engender fun, passion, and love from 19 November 2019, through 3 January 2020, ensuring you will have a grand holiday season for fun and love.

Your 2019 MacGuffin: You may need new workout clothes and sneakers to keep you motivated.

5 LEO
July 23 – Aug. 22

In 2019, you will be the celestial favourite for finding true love. If you are single and hoping to find lasting love, this is the year to circulate and to be open to a wide variety of types. Jupiter will remain in your fifth house of true love and romance until 2 December. This is the first time in over a decade you have had this generous planet working so hard for you to have an outstanding year of happiness.

If you have found your one true love, this would be an ideal year to become engaged or married, and the 20 January 2019 lunar eclipse in Leo could set a major life decision about a relationship in motion.

If you are already married, draw up new goals to work on together. There is a good chance you will be able to travel to at least one exciting foreign location for an awe-inspiring trip. Travel will be only one of many joyous possibilities to enjoy this year with the one you love.

This fifth house, where all your luck will be centred, also rules pregnancy and birth, so this would be a wonderful year to have a baby. If you have had problems with conception, see a fertility expert and take advantage of the positive rays Jupiter is sending you. While there's no guarantee you will conceive, careful research and finding the best medical facility for you will greatly increase your chance of success.

Finally, Mars will enter Leo on 1 July for a new two-year chapter. Because Mercury will be retrograde at the time, wait until 1 August to 17 August for any big announcements and launches. Happily, Venus will be in Leo from 27 July until 21 August, increasing your charm and making your ideas irresistible. The time near your birthday will indeed be special.

Your 2019 MacGuffin: A baby rattle. I think Leo sign Princess Meghan Markle will get pregnant soon, but it won't be announced to the public until later this year. Baby to be born in 2019.

6 VIRGO
Aug. 23 – Sept. 22

This will be a big, expansive year to improve your living quarters, especially if buying, selling or leasing property. If you're not be ready to do anything that dramatic and would rather renovate your kitchen or bath, paint several rooms of your house, or do extensive repairs, and 2019 will be your year to do it.

The reason for this cheerful news is that Jupiter, the giver of gifts and luck, recently entered Sagittarius, your fourth house of home, and will stay almost all year, until 2 December. This is the first time you have hosted Jupiter in your sector of home and family in 12 years. Under this rare trend, if you want to make changes, don't settle for anything less than finding and creating your dream living space. If the first few options you consider don't excite you, keep looking. This is meant to be your big reward in 2019, not to come again until October 2030.

Saturn, the great teacher planet, is moving through your fifth house of love and children, so it is clear that you will be focused mainly on your private life in 2019. Saturn won't leave your house of true love until December 2020, but hang in there. What you achieve with Saturn you will keep forever — and that could be your one true love.

If you have a baby in 2019, Saturn's presence suggests you may find having a child the hardest work you will ever do — but will give you the greatest happiness you will ever experience. You are a master juggler, Virgo, and

you also are a mutable sign, known to be exceptionally flexible and adaptable.

You will end 2019 in a heavenly state. On 27 December, Jupiter, giver of gifts and luck, will conjunct the Sun, making it the luckiest day of the year. By December, your love life will be showing enormous growth, for Jupiter will enter your true love sector for the first time in over a decade.

You may get engaged or married in the days surrounding 27 December, 2019 — in time for New Year's. Wow! What a joyous time you will have to look forward to in 2020.

Your 2019 MacGuffin: An elegant high tech vacuum cleaner for your new apartment or house. Virgo loves to keep things neat and tidy.

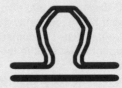

7 LIBRA
Sept. 23 – Oct. 22

As you begin 2019, Jupiter, the giver of gifts and luck, will be in Sagittarius, the sign Jupiter rules, so this planet will be in exceptionally strong position to bring happy experiences. He has not been in this position since late 2006–2007. Your Libra Sun is in an air sign and Sagittarius is a fire sign, signs that are compatible, so you will easily absorb the good fortune that Jupiter has for you. In 2019, Jupiter will open up your schedule to a lighter, breezier one than you had last year.

You will likely travel more than you have in recent years. Your trips will not take you too far away — within 200 miles — yet they will yield the most fun, and you will enjoy a touch of luxury, too. Face-to-face meetings with those out of town clients will pay off.

This will be a year that will underscore your skills in communication, so if you work in any aspect of publishing, broadcasting, marketing, public relations, social media, telecommunications, app or software development, or work with the post office, express mail services or messenger services, you will do exceedingly well. Regardless of what industry you are in, however, you will shine in 2019, as Jupiter won't leave Sagittarius until 2 December 2019. If you are renovating, it may take longer than expected. The same will apply if you are trying to sell property, and your broker may recommend you take the house off the market until real estate conditions improve. If you must sell, keep expectations reasonable. This is not a year you will likely make a killing in real estate, not unless your natal chart has Virgo rising.

On Christmas Day, 25 December, a new moon eclipse will appear in Capricorn, and this will likely be a peach. Each year the luckiest day of the year is when the Sun meets Jupiter in conjunction, and these two sparkling heavenly bodies always meet a different sign. On 27 December, every sign will feel happiness in a different way, but for you, dear Libra, happiness will come from home and family.

Your 2019 MacGuffin: A pair of hip sunglasses to keep in the car and make all that driving a little more comfortable.

8   SCORPIO
Oct. 23 – Nov. 22

Last year, 2018, was your wonder year. You were very busy taking advantage of opportunities that came up, and the seeds you planted last year will likely bring a bountiful financial harvest this year, 2019. The ventures you started from October 2017 to 2 December 2018, while Jupiter was in Scorpio, was very potent time for you, and appear to be the ventures that will pay off most abundantly.

Jupiter is now in Sagittarius, the sign it rules, so Jupiter is comfortable in this sign, and he will now light your house of earned income from the very start of the year to 2 December 2019. Your prospects are clear: this coming year is likely to be the most financially rewarding in 12 years. You will soon start to see income opportunities sprouting up around you, and remarkably, you will find yourself in the right place at the right time to take full advantage.

Another hint of where your money may emanate in 2019 is through publishing or broadcasting. It's true the media went through a tough time from December 2014 to December 2017, and publishing and broadcasting companies

that fell by the wayside won't be back. The magazines that did refresh their editorial will have a strong chance to flourish and to become even stronger than before. Network television and online video will also enter into a robust, golden age, with more program choices for audiences than ever. If you work in publishing or broadcasting, you have reason to be optimistic.

Even so, you may feel that either a client or management is not being realistic or not fully understanding the subtle nuances of a particular situation. You may feel your reputation is at stake, so you must defend your position and clarify the details. Fortunately Jupiter, planet of gifts and luck, will orbit with Venus, another financial planet, so your income will be firmly protected.

If you need to sign a contract, do it on the luckiest day of 2019, 27 December, when Jupiter conjoins the Sun. Your agreement will likely produce buckets of cash, and you will be showered with treasures from heaven.

Your 2019 MacGuffin: A new investment wrist watch to remind yourself this is your time of financial reward.

9   SAGITTARIUS
Nov. 23 – Dec. 21

You have worked long and hard, and now you are entering a glorious year of reward in just about every area of your life. You are about to see growth in love, romance, in regard to children and relationships, as well as impressive progress in career, health, and travel.

At the end of last year, on 7 November 2018, Jupiter, your ruling planet, entered Sagittarius for the first time since 24 November 2006. This year, 2019, should be one of the best years of your life. Jupiter won't leave Sagittarius until 2 December 2019, a period of nearly 11 months, so you truly do have a long time to enjoy what's to come.

Ancient astrologers wrote that if single, having Jupiter in one's sign, as you do now, would be the very sweetest time to meet your one true love. You, of course, must do your part to circulate socially to make that first con-

nection. Additionally, you'll have sexy Mars, the planet of action, on your side!

With Jupiter in your sign, you will find that your health improves. If you have a medical concern and wonder how Jupiter could be helpful, as you do your research, he will help you find a distinguished doctor who will understand your condition and who can help you. You have every reason to feel optimistic about your financials. On 2 December, Jupiter will move into your second house of earned income. The very area that gave you concern will be your most fortunate. This sensational outlook for earned income will stretch until 18 December 2020, so stay upbeat.

27 December will bring the luckiest day of 2019, when good-fortune Jupiter will meet with the mighty Sun. For you, this day will be purely financial, and you will find yourself at the right place at precisely the right time. If you need to sign a contract, this would be the day. This day arrives very close to the Christmas Day, 25 December eclipse, giving it a shimmering brilliance. You have a wonderful close to the year, and you will enter 2020 with renewed confidence, with much to show in terms of growth in just about every corner of your life.

Your 2019 MacGuffin: A small, powerful camera to use on your overseas trips in 2019.

10   CAPRICORN
Dec. 22 – Jan. 19

You are a very ambitious soul, Capricorn, and continually strive to see progress and growth in your career — your sign epitomizes leadership. Plato wrote that Capricorn is a philosopher king: wise in making decisions and caring of those in his employ. Let's look at your professional life, which is always a main interest for a Capricorn.

Jupiter moved into Sagittarius in November 2018 and is now in your twelfth house, helping you behind closed doors. Uranus' move into fellow earth sign Taurus will turn you into an idea factory from March 2019 and continue for seven glorious years. This is a once-in-a-lifetime trend, and one you are sure to enjoy.

In 2019 you will begin the process of making more room in your life, for you are soon to welcome Jupiter, the good-fortune planet, to Capricorn — a once-in-12-year event that will begin on 2 December 2019, and continue throughout 2020, crowning you the queen of the zodiac. Get ready for romance, superb career and money advancement, better health, and at least one opportunity to travel to an exciting city abroad.

On 27 December, we have the annual meeting of the Sun and good-fortune Jupiter, producing the Luckiest Day of the Year. On this day, you will be able to decide what is most important to you and to take steps toward making your dream a reality. It would be a perfect day to sign a contract, become engaged, or wed.

The glow of 27 December, a Friday, will continue into the following day, Saturday. The Sun, new moon, Jupiter, Saturn, and Pluto — half the solar system — will all be in Capricorn, and all will be favouring you. Uranus will send a lightning bolt of happiness, Neptune will send the gift of love, and Mars will have you surrounded by friends.

As celestial favourite, you will have your moment to step into the spotlight and on the world stage. The audience will be waiting and enthusiastically clapping hands for you — what will you say, dear Capricorn? It will be time to sing the song in your heart, for you will have the force of the universe behind you to make a dream dear to you come true.

Your 2019 MacGuffin: A wall mirror for the foyer to check your appearance before you leave the house.

11 AQUARIUS
Jan. 20 – Feb. 19

Last year you made a number of savvy career moves while Jupiter, the giver of gifts and luck, toured your solar tenth house of fame and honours. You may not yet realize that a majority of the decisions you made were precisely on target. Happily, you will see the truth of this in the coming year as events unfold. You worked hard last year, but this year will be easier and more fun.

Jupiter moved to Sagittarius late last year (7 November 2018) to stay until 2 December 2019. Fire-sign Sagittarius blends beautifully with your air-sign element of Aquarius, so you will absorb all the goodness that Jupiter has for you quite easily. In Sagittarius, Jupiter will light your eleventh house of friendship and events. Fascinating new people will pour into your life at a rapid rate. One or two will click perfectly with you and will become close friends.

You won't have to work as formally as you did last year. This year will have you out and about more often, meeting new people, and accomplishing just as much as you did when stayed stuck to your computer. In 2019, it won't be what you know but who you know that will move you ahead now.

Go to industry parties, and bring business cards. Join a club that keeps members informed on important developments related to your industry.

Send in an application to a club that interests you — it should be social, like a country club, or in cities, something like Soho House or the Groucho Club in London. Any time a group meets for a singular purpose, it's an eleventh house matter, and this is the area of your chart that is dazzlingly bright for your personal growth.

At the close of 2019, there is one spectacular event due that might influence your love life, if you are single — the conjunction of Mercury, ruler of your house of true love, with benefic Jupiter, operative from 31 December 2018, to 2 January 2020. This alignment could produce a dazzling engagement or wedding under the fireworks of New Year's Eve to welcome 2020. Keep the dream in your heart — 2019 will be a special year for you.

Your 2019 MacGuffin: A crystal vase from a distinguished retailer to hold fresh flowers, to celebrate and remind you of the good work you are doing for a charity or humanitarian concern.

12 PISCES
Feb. 20 – Mar. 20

You are about to enter into a spectacular career year, and soon your name will be in lights on the big marquee. You've been working hard in the years leading to 2019, and naturally have hoped your work would be recognized and applauded. You've done your preparation; here come the rewards. Jupiter, the giver of gifts and luck, a planet that expands opportunity and financial profits, is now in Sagittarius, your solar tenth house of honours, awards, and achievement, and shining like a beacon at the lofty pinnacle point in your horoscope. Jupiter will stay in Sagittarius nearly all year, until 2 December 2019.

Your tenth house governs your reputation and esteem that you are accorded from peers and VIPs in your industry or from the world at large. If your industry has award shows, enter as many as you can in 2019 for this is your year.

Neptune rules Pisces, but in ancient days, Pisces' ruling planet was Jupiter (Neptune was discovered in 1846). Today, astrologers look at the positions of both Jupiter and Neptune to decide your outlook for any given year.

As you enter 2019, you have two very special days to look forward to for excellent financial news: 22 January and 24 November 2019. On each of these days, Venus will align with Jupiter. Uranus, planet of surprise, will also send good news to you in the form of a welcome thunderbolt of lightning and likely bring you a large chunk of money.

Will this be a year of all work and no fun? Oh no — you will have fun too. At year's end Jupiter will enter your friendship sector and begin to draw many new faces to your circle. This year, the luckiest day of the year will fall on 27 December, showering you with happiness. Plan to do something special on that day. At the very least, you might sign a contract.

Also, look to New Year's Eve, for it is due to be the start of the best and most memorable decade for you. Will you get engaged or married as the fireworks light up the sky? You might! The world is your oyster, dear Pisces.

Your 2019 MacGuffin: A beautiful pen (Mont Blanc). You will be signing a contract on at least one (or more) major deals. You will also need to sign checks and send handwritten thank you notes to people who always believed in you and helped you get to where you are today.

3.
TO BUBBLE

Eco-warriors, Italian mamas, Metabolist manifestos, counter-cultural containers. From the Cénotaphe by Boullée to the Suitaloon by Archigram, the balls in Part 3 come disguised as domes, globes, spheres, balloons, orbs and bubbles.

Aerial view of Biosphere 2, Oracle, USA. Photo Visions of America/Getty Images, 1992

THEATRE OF POSSIBILITIES

Three decades ago, eight 'terranauts' walked into a gigantic eco-futurist vivarium called Biosphere 2 and survived for two years, beaten not by a lack of resources but by infighting, tensions, politics and disputes.

Text by Jack Self

Biospherians before their enclosure, April 1990. From left: Bernd Zabel, Linda Leigh, Taber MacCallum, Mark Van Thillo, Sally Silverstone, Roy Walford and Jayne Poynter. Photo Philippe Plailly/Science Photo

Biospherians tending crops inside the agriculture biome of Biosphere 2, 1991. Photo Peter Menzel/Science Photo

Biospherian Linda Leigh conducts a plant survey in the desert biome of Biosphere 2, 1991. Photo Peter Menzel/Science Photo

The colourful deserts of New Mexico were once populated by the Anasazi and Pueblo, native civilizations that thrived amidst the yucca and cacti. These peoples were ultimately erased by Spanish invaders, who were in turn displaced by British colonialists. With the discovery of gold, entrepreneurial prospectors flooded the state. Hardy townships sprung up, and oil men followed closely behind. The Rio Grande was dammed and diverted, creating vast tracts of fertile land at the feet of yellow mesas.

By the 1960s, this dream-like landscape had become the stage set for a strange and fantastical exploration of humanity's place in the universe. The US government was testing atomic weapons capable of destroying entire Soviet cities. Hippies were setting up communes, espousing an eco-friendly, anti-consumerist counterculture. NASA was preparing the Apollo astronauts, launching space rockets and mocking-up lunar landing sites. The deserts hosted two diametrically opposed worldviews, one that harnessed ultra-high-tech systems to destroy or escape the Earth, while another sought to protect the planet in off-grid townships of mud

Allen and Harding shared a messianic belief that humanity's future lay in colonizing other planets

brick and free love. These two ideologies rarely engaged with each other directly — unless you count UFO sightings as a form of communication between mystics and the military.

One significant exception to this is Biosphere 2, whose story begins in 1969 at an ecovillage outside Santa Fe. The Synergia Ranch was founded by John Allen (an ex-scientist specializing in metal alloys) and his long-time partner Marie Harding (an artist and photographer). The couple shared a deep commitment to environmental sustainability, and an almost messianic belief that humanity's future lay in colonizing other planets. They founded an artistic troupe at the Ranch called the Theatre of Possibilities, which used role-play to speculate on alternative presents and potential futures. One recurring science fiction scenario revolved around vivariums — self-contained artificial ecosystems capable of sustaining extraterrestrial human life on Mars, the Moon and during interstellar transit.

Within the first few months of its existence, the Ranch had attracted more than a dozen residents, including a man called Ed Bass. This Dallas billionaire had inherited oil money, but after graduating from Yale became disaffected by mainstream society. He drifted around from Nepal and Afghanistan to Greece and China, somehow eventually ending up in New Mexico. Here, the charismatic Allen drew him into the Ranch's circle. He convinced Bass to bankroll a US $150m complex of colossal spaceframe ziggurat vivariums. Together, they formed the Institute of Ecotechnics to pursue the idea, and spent the next decade conducting preparatory research — engaging all manner of expert scientists and consultants, including the Director of Kew Gardens Ghillean Prance. 'Their interest in science is not genuine,' he said in a 1983 interview. 'They seem to have some sort of secret agenda, they seem to be guided by some sort of religious or philosophical system.'

In 1984, Bass and Allen established a joint venture company Space Biosphere Ventures, and formally launched Biosphere 2. Marie, who had just returned from the first modern Western expedition to Szechwan province, and was completing a film about the archi-

tecture of Iran while training to become a
Karate black belt, became Vice President of
Finance. A piece of land was acquired in
Oracle, Arizona and construction began
in 1987.

Biosphere 2 remains the largest vivarium ever constructed, and its hermetically
sealed interior is more than 13,000 m2
(equal to about forty Boeing 747s). Above
ground, there are six primary ecosystem
enclosures: 1,900 m2 of tropical rainforest,
850 m2 of ocean (including a coral reef),
450 m2 of mangrove swamp, 1,300 m2 of
savannah grasslands, 1,400 m2 of fog desert
and a 2,500 m2 agricultural compound with
laboratories and living quarters for 8–10
'biospherians' (also sometimes called terranauts). Electricity comes from an industrial
gas power plant. Under the ground, a complicated network of ducts and utilities
allow for precise control of the ecosystem
variables; carbon scrubbers, heaters,
dehumidifiers and air conditioners control
atmospheric conditions. During the day,
heat in the greenhouses causes the air
volume to massively expand, while at night
it cools and contracts — to accommodate
this fluctuation, two massive accordion
'lungs' contain the overflow. Various species,
from insects to small mammals, were
packed into each environment. After four
years, the vivarium was poised like a
wound watch.

On 26 September 1991, eight terranauts
sealed themselves inside Biosphere 2
and did not come out for almost two years.
During this time the only contact was by
telephone and CCTV, with no material
(not even air) entering or exiting the system.
For the first twelve months, the biospherians suffered quite badly. The oxygen levels
dropped to a dangerously low level, making
the terranauts constantly drowsy and irrita-
ble. The farm produced bananas, papayas,
sweet potatoes, beets, peanuts, rice and
wheat. However, it did not produce enough
food, and a low-calorie diet saw the average
terranaut lose 16% of their body mass.
The rainforest and mangrove flourished, but
the fog desert became too humid. The ocean
needed periodic intervention to maintain
pH balance, but overall it was healthy,
and the corals reproduced. Unfortunately,
most of the insects died, while cockroaches

and ants overran every ecosystem. More
problematically, the hungry biospherians
had split into two rival factions that were
barely on speaking terms. One group, led by
Jane Poynter, advocated for importing food
into the system. They believed the ability to
conduct research was more important than
maintaining total closure. The rival group,
led by Abigail Alling, argued the opposite:
that Biosphere 2 must remain a perfectly
contained experiment. Rising tensions came
to a head when the Poynter faction con-
ducted a night raid on seed stocks, gorging
themselves. Poynter was subsequently fired,
but refused to leave the compound — cor-
rectly guessing that there was no one who
would be prepared for break the seal. Over
the next year, the crew struggled on with
their experiments and infighting. Eventually,
they were forced to inject oxygen into the
carbon-saturated ecosystems. They also had
to evacuate an injured terranaut, who was
accused of smuggling food into Biosphere 2
when they returned. Coverage by the press
was intense, with mixed reports from inside
the Biosphere combining with misunder-
standing about the project ambitions. The

*The world of eco-futurism had tussled
with high-tech capitalism, and neither
had come off well*

The Biospherians on closure day entering the front airlock, September 1991. From left: Sally Silverstone, Abigail Alling, Roy Walford, Taber MacCallum, Jane Poynter, Linda Leigh, Mark Nelson. Courtesy John Adams

result was public controversy and confusion. *Time* magazine wrote, 'the veneer of credibility, already bruised by allegations of tamper-prone data, secret food caches and smuggled supplies, has cracked... the two-year experiment in self-sufficiency is starting to look less like science and more like a $150 million stunt'.

After a brief intermission to recalibrate the ecosystems (and exterminate the cockroaches and ants), a second mission was announced in March 1994. By June, disagreements between Bass and Allen about the future of the project became untenable. A series of power moves unfolded quite quickly, which resulted in the collapse of funding. Bass seems to have lost the faith: not only did he dissolve Space Biosphere Ventures, but he called in Steve Bannon to administer the liquidation of Biosphere 2. The hapless terranauts were not told about the external chaos, and continued to monitor and manage the vivarium. Three months later, terranauts from the first mission broke into the compound and gained access to one of the greenhouses, communicating with the crew and terminating the mission.

Legal battles continued to swirl around Biosphere for a further decade, but in essence the experiment was dead: killed not by scientific concerns (the second mission had attained oxygen stability and improved crop yield) but by crew in-fighting, psychological tensions, power politics, and disputes over how the project should be managed. The world of eco-futurism had tussled with high-tech capitalism, and neither had come off well. Ultimately, Biosphere 2 is a lesson — as if one needed it — in the sad reality that in overcoming the basic struggle with nature for existence, humanity has become its own worst enemy.

Kiyoshi Awazu, Metabolism logo, 1960

METABOLISM,

MOVEMENT, 　　　　　　　　　　MANKIND

Searching for new beginnings after the devastation of war, the Metabolists embraced the sphere as one of the building blocks to shape the future of Japan.

Text by Christine Bjerke

Shoji Hayashi, *Ricoh Pavillon*, Expo '70, Osaka, 1970. Photo Architectural Press Archive/RIBA

Taro Okamoto, *Tower of the Sun*, Expo '70 Festival Plaza, Osaka, 1970. Photo Architectural Press Archive/RIBA

Kiyonori Kikutake, *Expo Tower*, Expo '70, Osaka, 1970. Courtesy Gary Holmes

As the shape suggests, the sphere — or open ball — can expand without end. It has no direction and is not static. It can be duplicated, rotated, and scaled up and down. It is also the shape architect Kenzo Tange and the Metabolist Movement took as a symbol for the rebuilding of post-war society in Japan in the late 1950s. In the wake of the devastation of war, what role did the sphere and the circle play in questioning both human and architectural vitality? How did it manifest itself metaphysically and physically in Japan and beyond?

FROM THE GALACTIC TO THE MOLECULAR

As the first non-Western avant-garde movement, Tange and his team of young designers were proposing much more than just a new architecture. The goal of the new ideology was to transform and reinvent a whole country. As architect Rem Koolhaas and curator Hans Ulrich Obrist documented in their book *Project Japan: Metabolism Talks*, where they interviewed the surviving visionaries behind Metabolism, the movement questioned the very fundamentals of Japanese society after World War II. The movement outlined its ambitions in its Metabolist manifesto, with a swirl logo designed by artist Kiyoshi Awazu on the first page. The logo was also the trademark of Metabolism and connected the work to the original meaning of the swirl, or *tomoe*, which means 'hoping' or 'wishing' in Japanese culture. This meaning exemplified the emotional ambitions for societal change and the movement's desire to create a better future. What the logo also did, beyond the historical bond, was to emphasize the importance of the biological cycle of Metabolism. And as stated in the manifesto: 'We regard human society as a vital process — a continuous development from atom to nebula. The reason why we use such a biological word, the metabolism, is that, we believe, design and technology should be a denotation of human vitality.'

The movement officially published two thousand copies of its vision document at the 1960 World Design Conference in Tokyo. It was entitled *Metabolism: The Proposals for New Urbanism* and consisted

Shigeo Fukuda, Expo '70 poster

of four essays: *Ocean City*, *Space City*, *Towards Group Form*, and *Material and Man*. As described by the team: 'We are not going to accept the metabolism as a natural historical process, but we are trying to encourage metabolic development of our society through our proposals.' Ranging in scale from the galactic to the molecular, the projects proposed by the movement addressed a varied portfolio, from large urban master plans to residential capsules.

The testbed for the radical proposals was the 1970 World Exposition in Osaka, the first expo to take place in Asia. With its title 'Progress and Harmony for Mankind', it presented numerous visions and designs behind Metabolism. Just like in the movement, Tange was the leading figure, responsible for the master plan of the entire exhibition site with its many flexible and temporary interventions, ranging in scale from towers to capsules. The centre of gravity for the expo was the 70-metre-tall Tower of the Sun by artist Taro Okamoto, its space frame penetrating the Big Roof by Tange on the Festival Plaza. Featuring a circular golden head that represented the future, the tower became the symbol of the expo and is one of the few surviving pieces today. Also overlooking the site was the Expo Tower by architect Kiyonori Kikutake, which was built using standardized components and could expand vertically. Attached to its side were a series of capsules that served various functions, among them information booth, VIP space and viewing platform. Another landmark, and the main ball at the expo, was the Ricoh Pavilion by architect Shoji Hayashi, a 40-metre-tall structure in the form of a huge balloon that, like the towers, could be seen from anywhere on the expo grounds. On display inside the 25-metre-diameter balloon were projectors and electronic devices. Among the exhibited objects were some of the early cell phones. Combining a spherical and organic space with items of technology, the movement showed how the body and architecture continuously negotiate with the future city.

Existing between the metaphysical and physical, the open ball assumed many shapes in Metabolist thinking. This diversity emphasized how the movement saw the post-war condition of the country not as an obstacle but as an opportunity. The exhibited projects at the Expo in Osaka not only heralded a new era for Japan but also looked at the world outside the country. From this stage, the Metabolists presented to the whole world their strategies for urbanization and architecture, and explored the impact of human ideology on the built environment. Following the 1960 World Design Conference and the interest from outside Japan, members of the Metabolist movement carried out projects in the Middle East and Africa.

REPRODUCE, GROW AND TRANSFORM

In various ways, the manifesto logo symbolized the Metabolist movement and represented the threefold division of *Man, Earth* and *Sky*. An essential aspect of this thinking was that cities and buildings should be able to reproduce, grow and transform in response to their environments. At the scale of the domestic, the Nakagin Capsule Tower in Tokyo by architect Kisho Kurokawa is celebrated as one of the built manifestations

Cities and buildings should be able to reproduce, grow and transform in response to their environments

of the movement. Completed in just thirty days in 1972, it presented a new technologically advanced architecture that could incorporate organic growth and respond to a city in constant flux. With its huge iconic disk windows in each plug-in housing unit, the tower was the world's first built work of capsular architecture. However, the design of the building was also heavily inspired by the traditional tea ceremony rooms and Japanese classics called *fukkō*, which means 'a return to the past'. Like a tea ceremony room, each capsule was designed as a self-contained space with its own metabolism. Built-in furniture means that everything — bed, storage cabinets, kitchen — had a fixed place. This spatial logic echoed the *chashitsu*, which characterizes the Japanese tea room, where the raised podium and preparation area are integrated into the space. In this sense the building presented an architecture that belonged to both the past and future. Despite its iconic status, the future of Nakagin Capsule Tower is uncertain. It is visibly decaying, and its residents have voted for it to be demolished.

Kisho Kurokawa, *Nakagin Capsule Tower*, Tokyo, 1972. Photo Architectural Press Archive/RIBA

Isamu Noguchi, *Moon World*, Expo '70, Osaka, 1970. Behind it is the *Tower of the Sun*.

Panasonic Time Capsule: contents, casting, examining the model by the Selection Committee and enclosure, 1970.
Courtesy Panasonic

ENCAPSULATING THE METABOLIC FUTURE

Although the projects by the Metabolists reflect a particular period, their contemporary relevance should not be ignored. Koolhaas and Obrist are not the only Western thinkers who have turned to the movement for inspiration. Tange and his team focused on metabolism in humans and architecture, an issue of relevance in light of today's increased need to respond to changing environmental conditions. Further, there is the question of identity, which in many ways seems to be the primary concern of Metabolism. With the Moon World sculptural ball built in 1970 on the edge of the expo site, artist Isamu Noguchi created a sphere that contained many disks. The sculpture represented how the larger projects by the Metabolist movement, such as the expo itself, linked with the smaller pavilions and vice-versa. In addition, the warm earthy colour and industrial metal of the ball expressed how Japan wanted to move forward while respecting tradition.

Most of the realized buildings by the Metabolists have been demolished over the past forty years, with just a few landmarks remaining. Besides the Tower of the Sun on the expo site, a handful of projects are preserved because of their architectural and cultural value. Apart from the few built works that still exist, we are also left with a time capsule donated by the Matsushita Electric Industrial Company (now known as Panasonic), to be left for 5,000 years and opened in the year 6970. Contained inside are 2,098 carefully curated objects that capture daily life in Japanese society in 1970. How the world will react to its contents one day is impossible to predict, but time will tell when the Metabolist Ball is opened 4,952 years from now.

Night-time view, Expo '70, Osaka, 1970. Photo Rolls Press/Popperfoto/Getty Images

RADICAL

Inspired by space travel and science fiction, a generation of designers dreamed up futuristic inflatables, allowing us to enter into a new relationship with the world.

Text by Kirsten Algera

Archigram's David Greene in inflatable mock-up of Suitaloon, Milan 1968. Photo Dennis Crompton. Courtesy Archigram Archives

BUBBLES

In 2005 German philosopher Peter Sloterdijk created a satirical installation for the *Making Things Public* exhibition at the Zentrum für Kunst und Medien in Karlsruhe. Inspired by the fragile peace in Afghanistan and Iraq, Sloterdijk proposed a 'pneumatic parliament', a transparent dome that could be pumped up within twenty-four hours in post-conflict regions, providing space for 160 democratic representatives. Democracy as an export product: Sloterdijk claimed that *The Pneumatic Parliament* offered 'the architectural conditions necessary for democratic processes, and as such forms a striking and futurist contribution to the worldwide distribution of Western democratic principles'.

Some saw Sloterdijk's sarcasm as a crass joke, but in fact it was a sequel to his philosophical trilogy *Spheres*, published between 1998 and 2004. In that work, with its total of 2,500 pages, Sloterdijk describes human beings as 'sphere builders', who try to give shape to the immensity of the world. They surround themselves with 'bubbles' (houses, gardens, parks, nations) to protect themselves. Sloterdijk's trilogy is not just a philosophical treatise but a series of books about space and architecture, or as Sloterdijk calls it '"sphereology" — the study of the human need for interior space'.

Inflatable spheres were conceived as spaces that could set people thinking forty years before Sloterdijk. Around 1965, the inflatable began its triumphal march through avant-garde art, popular culture and alternative architecture. The pneumatic 'bubble' owed its popularity not only to the technological innovation and space travel of the mid-20th century, but also and above all to the search by countercultural movements for anarchistic ways of building and living. Ironically, the alternative 'Pneu World' was made possible in large part by the military-industrial complex in the United States.

Rudimentary inflatables were designed as far back as 1946, by Walter Bird and the Cornell Aeronautical Laboratory, to protect the US Army's radar antennae. Known as 'radomes', they caught on because they could be constructed quickly and moved easily, and they offered protection against the elements in the form of an inflatable plastic shell. The US government invested in Bird's design from 1946 onwards, and hundreds of radomes were built in the 1950s. Bird developed his inflatable technology with military money, but like many engineers in mid-century America, he made his profits in the civilian world. In 1956 he set up Birdair Structures, Inc. to sell inflatable sheds, greenhouses

and swimming-pool roofs to residents of the suburbs of New York. He did a roaring trade, and Bird's plastic miracle attracted the attention of architects. In the late 1950s he was present at the birth of experiments with inflatable domes, rather like German engineer Frei Otto, who had designed an inflatable structure that could withstand the harsh Antarctic climate, and American architect Buckminster Fuller, who designed a dome to protect Manhattan.

Interest in bubble architecture took off alongside progress in space travel and the popularity of the science-fiction genre. Inventive technologies for zero gravity, whether mid-city, mid-air or underwater, were being imagined just as such things were becoming possible. Pneumatic technology advanced and gave bubbles sci-fi credibility. The bubble was suddenly the ideal residential environment of the postwar era. Such technologies also had a major influence on a new generation of experimental architects and designers in the late 1960s and early 1970s. The combination of lightweight materials and moveable spaces fitted perfectly with ideas about a radically different, more social concept of design, in which individuals would be able to reconfigure their own environments and enter into a new relationship with the world. In those years Achizoom in Italy, Art Farm in San Francisco, Archigram in the United Kingdom, French artist François Dallegret, Italian Ettore Sottsass and the Austrian group Coop Himmelb(l)au and designer Walter Pichler took to designing futuristic, plastic inflatables to give a new interpretation to existing ideas about architecture.

The bubble became the pars pro toto of a utopian counterculture. In contrast to its use in the suburbs of New York, it was not deployed as protection against a hostile outside world but as a more socially and environmentally conscious architectural element that could conjure up experiences and bind with that world — just as Peter Sloterdijk, in the third volume of *Spheres (Foams)* describes how since the Enlightenment our pluralistic world no longer needs a 'monosphere' but instead bubbles that interconnect to become foam.

Radome, c. 1945. Photo Hulton Archive/Getty Images

BUCKMINSTER FULLER, SHOJI SADAO, CLOUD NINE, 1960. COURTESY THE ESTATE OF R. BUCKMINSTER FULLER

RICHARD BUCKMINSTER FULLER, CLOUD NINE, 1960

In 1960 it struck architect Richard Buckminster Fuller as a good idea to cover central Manhattan with a huge inflatable dome three kilometres in diameter. The structure would stretch from the East River to the Hudson, and from 21st Street to 64th Street. The idea was to shut residents off from the outside world completely and by doing so, Buckminster Fuller claimed, to offer them free climate control in summer and winter and keep the air healthy. 'The cost saving in ten years would pay for the dome. Domed cities are going to be essential to the occupation of the Arctic and the Antarctic,' he wrote.

In that same period, Buckminster Fuller designed what he called *Cloud Nines*, communities that would dwell in extremely lightweight spheres, with a polyethylene outer skin. Each sphere would be a mile (1.6 km) wide and capable of housing several thousand people. He believed they could be kept inflated by the warming of the air inside. His surface-to-volume calculations showed that the structural weight of a dome with a diameter of half a mile (0.8 km) would be one thousandth the weight of the air it contained. When trapped solar energy and human activity heated the air inside just one degree above the surrounding air temperature, the sphere would float like a hot air balloon. A skinned, one-mile-diameter sphere could easily support itself and several thousand people and their property. *Cloud Nines* would migrate like birds from place to place, or settle on mountaintops, enabling people 'to converge and deploy around Earth without its depletion'. Not that Buckminster Fuller was overly concerned about the future of the planet. He faced the future with optimism. 'When world realization of its unlimited wealth has been established there as yet will be room for the whole of humanity to stand indoors in greater New York City, with more room for each human than at an average cocktail party,' he wrote in his 1969 essay *Operating Manual for Spaceship Earth*.

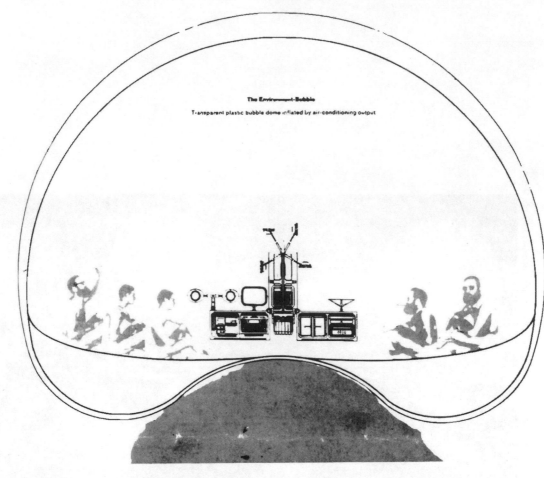

THE ENVIRONMENT BUBBLE, ART IN AMERICA, APRIL 1965. COURTESY F. DALLEGRET

GOOD GOD/NUDITY, 1965. PHOTO MARC LULLIER. COURTESY F. DALLEGRET

**FRANÇOIS DALLEGRET,
UN-HOUSE. TRANSPORTABLE
STANDARD-OF-LIVING PACKAGE/
ENVIRONMENT BUBBLE, 1965**

In the 1960s, artist and designer François Dallegret called himself 'GOD & Co' — by his own account a name derived from 'Go Dallegret!' — and 'Aestheticien ACID', the latter an acronym, according to Dallegret, of 'Association of Canadian Industrial Designers'. He was impossible to pigeonhole, as the magazine *Art in America* made clear in a 1966 article about his 'art fiction': 'He imagines that soon most human activity will occur not on earth but in space. The artist of the future differs from his predecessors, however, in that he creates no material objects, but rather makes environments in space, which induce a variety of specific sensory reactions in the people who enter them.' Dallegret himself described this as a future in which the artist 'will create all sorts of natural and supernatural feelings we don't know about yet. It will kill Descartes, this thing. And Braque.'

Dallegret presented his 'art fiction' in a wide range of media: graphic design, product design, interiors, drawings and installations. It was a futuristic universe that in the 21st century has largely ceased to be fiction and has become technological reality. Which helps to explain why Dallegret's 1965 drawing *The Environment Bubble* was constructed for real three years ago for a festival in Montreal. Dallegret initially created the design as one of six 'architectural' drawings for *A Home is Not a House*, an essay by British architecture critic Reyner Banham. 'When your house contains such a complex of piping, flues, ducts, wires, lights, inlets, outlets, ovens, sinks, refuse disposers, hi-fi reverberators, antennae, conduits, freezers, heaters — when it contains so many services that the hardware could stand up by itself without any assistance from the house, why have a house to hold it up?' Banham asks. In the drawing *Un-House. Transportable Standard-of-Living Package/Environment Bubble*, Dallegret proposes a moveable set of equipment, housed in an inflatable bubble with solar panels. In the drawing the bubble is enlivened by nude portraits of Banham and Dallegret. Or actually, as Dallegret explained later, of the designer and a body double for Banham. 'I decided that if you were going to live in a bubble you had to be completely naked. You didn't care about having a fancy suit or wearing a funny tie because everything is already inside the bubble. While I was doing the drawings, I thought Banham would have to join me inside the bubble — but, he didn't want to pose naked! So, I took my body and simply put his head on top of it.'

ARCHIGRAM (MICHAEL WEBB), SUITALOON, 1968

In 1961, strongly influenced by pop art, science fiction comics and technologies developed during the Cold War, architects' collective Archigram imagined a new relationship between the individual and the city. 'We are seeking the Living City,' the avant-garde collective wrote. It drew large, mobile infrastructures (such as a 'walking' city on telescopic legs that strides across the landscape), which could adjust to continually changing circumstances.

Unlike other radical architects of the 1960s, Archigram was not so much campaigning against modernity as wanting to accelerate it; architecture ought to make more of an effort to keep up with changes in the fields of technology, products and lifestyle. 'The fundamental characteristics of futuristic architecture will be expendability and transience,' the collective wrote. 'Our house will last less time than we do; every generation must make its own city.' It turned against the 'conservative' belief that buildings are meant to be static entities. As an alternative, the group proposed mobile, technology-rich cities and portable homes like the *Suitaloon*, a suit that covers all of life's basic necessities and can become an inflatable chamber.

In 1968 the group developed a prototype, based on an earlier design from 1966. The idea was that the *Suitaloon*, like Dallegret's *Environment Bubble*, would contain all that was needed for a nomadic life: electricity, water, a shell and a connection with other *Suitaloons*. 'Each suit has a plug serving a similar function to the key to your front door,' group member Michael Webb explained. 'You can plug into your friend and you will both be in one envelope, or you can plug into any envelope, stepping out of your suit, which is left clipped onto the outside ready to step into when you leave. The plug also serves as a means of connecting envelopes together to form larger spaces.' Back to the future: *Suitaloon* could be seen as an illustration of an idea not described until fifty years later, that of society as a concatenation of bubbles (see page 138 Peter Sloterdijk, Foams).

WALTER PICHLER, GROßER RAUM, 1967

'We must liberate architecture from building,' wrote Viennese architects Hans Hollein and Walter Pichler in 1962 in their manifesto *Absolute Architecture*. In texts, sketches and small-scale architecture they left no doubt about their aversion to post-war functionalism. The pair believed that the goal of architecture was not functionality but 'a ritual expression of sublime pointlessness'. In the late 1960s, Walter Pichler elaborated on this in a series called 'Prototypes', with which he participated in the fourth Documenta exhibition. His hybrids of art and design were, he said, a means of ensuring 'that architecture be free from the constraints of construction and that sculpture be free from the limits of abstraction'.

Großer Raum was one of those prototypes, an inflatable reminiscent of Dallegret's *Un-House*. In this case, however, the bubble was not filled with multi-media equipment but with two mysterious objects, the *Kleiner Raum* (Small Room) and the *Fernsehhelm – Tragbares Wohnzimmer* (TV Helmet – Portable Living Room). These were carefully constructed prototypes of equipment intended for mass production. The *Kleiner Raum*

was a helmet that turned the wearer's head into a kind of ultra-modern radio receiver, consisting of two large balls. With the help of an integrated microphone, the voice of the wearer could be amplified by an external loudspeaker system. Without being seen, he or she could observe the surroundings through two small holes. The TV helmet was precisely the opposite, in that the wearer was completely cut off from the world around and could see only the small screen; here was Marcuse's 'One-Dimensional Man'. With the prototypes, Pichler said, he was exploring 'the emotional qualities of architecture'. 'A building might tell a story, rather than just be a function. What I call for is an architecture which fascinates.'

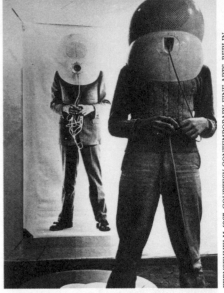

FERNSEHHELM, 1967. COURTESY CONTEMPORARY FINE ARTS, BERLIN

ETTORE SOTTSASS, STADIUM WITH LARGE HABITABLE LEVELS FOR THE CAREFUL OBSERVATION OF THE WATER AND THE SKY, 1972

From 1972 onwards the already famous Italian designer Ettore Sottsass published a series of drawings in Italian design magazines portraying the world as a festival. In *The Planet as a Festival*, work and social conditioning are replaced by free time; buildings have broken free of their urban environment and moved to deserts, jungles, rivers or ravines. Sottsass proposes deploying technology and architecture to expand our self-consciousness and live in harmony with nature. Liberated from 'the insane, sick, dangerous and aggressive idea that men must live only to work and must work to produce and then to consume', individuals can 'come to know by means of their bodies, their psyche, and their sex, that they are living'.

Drawings like *A Dispenser of Incense, LSD, Marijuana, Opium,* *Laughing Gas*, in which an enormous phallus emits intoxicants above a campsite that looks like a festival, and *Temple for Erotic Dances*, with pavilions in the shape of genitals, show that the journey through India that Sottsass had made a short time before made a lasting impact on him. The rituals and the animist character of places or buildings are unmistakably Indian influences.

The lens-shaped perspex *Stadium with Large Habitable Levels for the Careful Observation of the Water and the Sky*, and indeed *Rafts for Listening to Chamber Music*, are an exhortation to look more closely at the environment. Sottsass himself called his drawings 'vague, but not utopian'; they were less a celebration of Indian rituals, or drugs, or a utopian vision than advocacy of an architecture that has freed itself from a functional programme. From now on, Sottsass wrote, architecture would be able to concern itself with rituals.

oped into a proposal for a series of *Pneumatische Wohneinheite* ('Pneumatic Living Units'). One of the units was a transparent bubble that stuck like a parasite onto the famous Museum Fridericianum in Kassel. Oase Nr. 7 ('Oasis No. 7') consisted of a steel-lattice armature installed on the museum's second story that functioned as a platform leading to a transparent bubble hung from the window. The interior, with its artificial palm trees, dangled precariously over the museum's car park.

The bubble was meant not just as a 'mind-expanding experience' but as a symbol of institutional criticism and an ecological project. Lauris Ortner, a member of Haus-Rucker-Co, explained: 'We were especially interested in attempts to find new spatial conditions that could not only effect stronger sensations, but also reduce the building materials needed. Spherical membranes, supported in their form by air pumped in, seemed to offer the best preconditions for this.' That experiments nowadays are forced to take account of health and safety concerns was recently demonstrated by an exhibition of the Haus-Rucker-Co's oeuvre in Berlin. Only one of the inflatable bubbles could actually be used. And not for long; at the opening a visitor slipped as she was getting into the bubble. Instead of heightened sensitivity, a broken leg.

HAUS-RUCKER-CO, OASE NR. 7, INSTALLATION AT DOCUMENTA 5, KASSEL, GERMANY, 1972

It is surely no accident that, in the city of Freud in the late 1960s, architects' collective Haus-Rucker-Co ('house movers') focused on a 'Mind-Expanding Programme' of art and architecture. It aspired to extend people's psycho-physical experiences through art and architecture projects, like the 1967 *Balloon for Two*, a transparent PVC membrane that inflated into a large bubble. Supported by a steel rack, the sphere projected into the street from the facade of an existing building. Inside, a man and a woman sat in two halves of a plastic bathtub. Haus-Rucker-Co declared:

'Our balloons will help you to discover an unknown feeling of tranquillity, of security, of relaxation. And love. We want to heighten your sensitivity.' A year later, the idea that a concentrated experience of space could offer a direct approach to changes in consciousness led to the construction of another pneumatic space capsule, called *Yellow Heart*. 'Through a lock made of three air rings, one arrives at a transparent plastic mattress,' Haus-Rucker-Co explained. 'Offering just enough space for two people, it projects into the centre of a spherical space that is made up of soft, air-filled chambers. The space pulsates at extended intervals.'

A few years later, *The Balloon for Two* and *Yellow Heart* were devel-

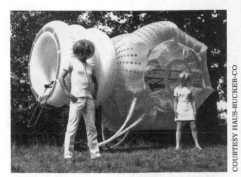

Haus-Rucker-Co, Yellow Heart, 1968

BALLPARK FIGURES

On the hunt for a miracle hangover cure, art students from the Rietveld Academie headed to the nearby Amsterdamse Bos for a spot of 'bubble football', a game guaranteed to make everything spin.

Photography by Guus Kaandorp

DELIRIOUS ARCHITECTS AND GLOBES

Text by Véronique Patteeuw

Inspired by the form of the earth, one shape has haunted architecture and its scientists, humanists and even utopians more than any other since time immemorial: the globe.

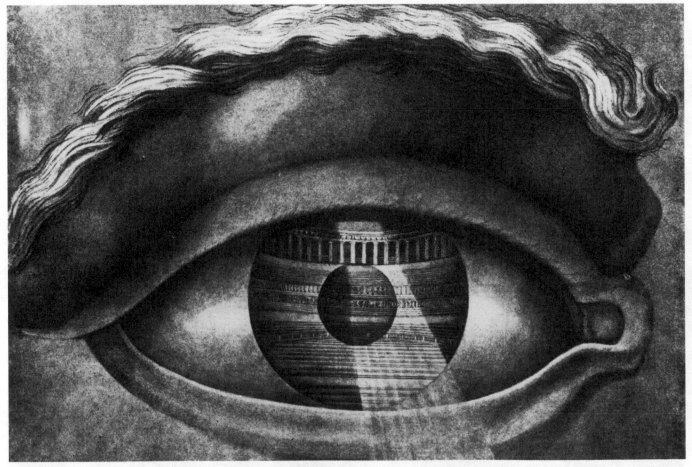

Claude-Nicolas Ledoux, *Oeil Reflétant l'Intérieur du Théâtre de Besançon*, 1784. Courtesy Bibliothèque Nationale de France

Perfectly shaped, shimmering from all sides
and holding an impeccable balance despite
the laws of gravity, the globe has been an
object of fascination throughout architectural history. If the sphere represents both
earth and the extra-terrestrial space of the
universe, within architectural history it
found itself at the crossroads of architecture
and astronomy, geography, philosophy,
science-fiction, entertainment, and even
Utopia. From the Roman Pantheon to
Boullée's cenotaph for Newton, and from
Buckminster Fuller's Biodome to OMA's
City of the Captive Globe, architects have
always been inspired by the shape of the
earth, fascinated by the universe.[1]

THE GODS AND THE GLOBE

When the Italian architect and surveyor
Giambattista Nolli drew his iconographic
plan of Rome in 1736, he presented all
interior spaces as public domain, displaying
the figure of the architecture and the
ground it claimed. In Nolli's plan, one building catches the observer's attention immediately: an ancient Roman temple with a
perfect circular plan. Thought to have been
designed by Apollodorus of Damascus in
around 125 for the emperor Hadrian, and
dedicated to all gods, the Roman Pantheon
astonishes by its impeccably balanced
interior: a vault that could house a perfect
sphere, of 43.3 metres (150 Roman feet) in
diameter. The presence of the (absent)
sphere produces a powerful spatial experience, enhanced by a giant eight-metre-
diameter oculus joining the cosmos to the
earth and the spiritual to the temporal. The
absent sphere is articulated by five rings of
sunken panels, evenly spaced in the ceiling
and a checkerboard floor that accentuated
the central geometric theme of circles
and squares.

The Roman pantheon was not the first
building that would use the form of the
sphere. Two centuries before, the Italian
agronomist Marcus Terentius Varro constructed an aviary in the form of a sphere.
Located in Casinum, near Rome, the complex, an enclosure with high walls and
netted roofs, recomposed a small paradise
with a spherical dome engraved with astral
signs used to measure time. Trees were

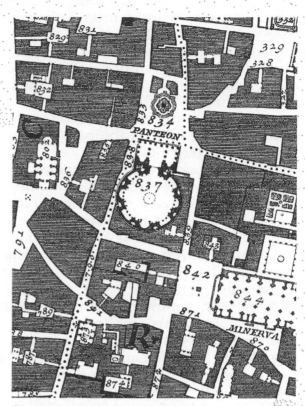

Giambattista Nolli, Detail from *La Nuova Topografia di Roma*, 1748

planted around a series of water features.
The complex was designed for guests who
frequented the building and came there to
dine. They experienced a device of contra-
dictions: on the one hand they saw birds in
well-lit cages all around them, on the other
ducks wading in a pond. In its centre, a
small island, which ancient astronomers
considered to be the middle of the world.
A tambourine-shaped table represented the
earth. Here again, circles and squares seem
to add to the spherical experience of the
Avery.

THE GLOBE AND
REVOLUTIONARY THOUGHT

Over time, scientists and artists imagined
globes so big that they became true architectural projects. One could argue that the
shape of the globe haunted architecture,
its scientists, its humanists and even its
utopians. The utopian aspect of the sphere
was fully explored in the 19th century, most
particularly by some of the leading architects of the Enlightenment[2], among them
the Frenchman Étienne-Louis Boullée

(1728–1799), whose large, monumental projects were especially influential. Although
Boullée mostly realized small works for
private and religious patrons, he emerged
during the French Revolution as a theoreti-
cian and teacher at the École Nationale des
Ponts et Chaussées and the Académie
Royale d'Architecture, where he conceived
of architecture as the possibility to construct
the moral conscience of man.[3]

For Boullée, architectural conception
came with a certain radicalism. Combining
Enlightenment philosophy, a profound love
of radical geometry and a fascination for
gigantic scale, Boullée imagined buildings
in which he removed all unnecessary orna-
mentation, inflated elementary volumes, and
favoured a distinctively abstract, geometric
style. Regularity, symmetry and variety were
the golden rules of his architecture.
Antiquity remained an important source,
mostly for the formal beauty it inspired, the
system of orders it imposed, and the con-
structive logic it allowed. But he proactively
used his fascination for historical prece-
dents to mix classical elements with
contemporary and hitherto unseen settings.
If one would describe Boullée as a revolutionary architect it would be for two reasons.
First, as an artist, Boullée criticized the
architecture of his time and proposed bold,
progressive and deliberately provocative
solutions to the accepted tradition. His
projects are often understood as utopian
because they envision a new society, and
to aspire a new sense of wellbeing for mankind. Second, Boullée also acted as a theore-
tician and elaborated important artistic
policies for some of the French Revolution's
new institutions. From 1789 on, he widened
the programmes of his projects to include
monuments inspired by the revolutionary
world: a national assembly, a municipal
palace, a cemetery and memorials.

Amongst these monuments, the cenotaph for Isaac Newton is probably Boullée's
most emblematic project. This funerary
monument, conceived by Boullée in 1784
and erected in memory of Isaac Newton,
consists of a 500-foot-diameter sphere
surrounded by a cylindrical pedestal. The
sphere seems to be floating and buried at
the same time. Three bases surrounding
the sphere hold the whole composition

*Architects have always been inspired
by the shape of the earth, fascinated
by the universe*

together and enable stairways to reach the
upper levels. The bases are planted with
curved lines of trees that accentuate the
relation between sphere and base, between
globe and earth. An excavated ground-level
passage enables visitors to arrive at the
centre of the sphere, where they can admire
from a pedestal a constellation of stars or
a gigantic clock. Indeed, two versions of the
Cenotaph project were designed: one with a
daylight-filled armillary sphere at the centre,
a thick vault and a wide esplanade around
the mausoleum; the other with a celestial
vault that becomes thinner at the top and
with a narrower base.

Boullée's pursuit of monumental architecture continued in such projects as the
Chapel for the death and the Cenotaph for
a warrior, a grave with the proportions of a
massive monument and a frieze made of
gigantic silhouettes of armed soldiers.
But most striking of all is his project for a
Public Library, a basilica with an immense
semi-circular vault with zenith lighting
above a central study and reading space.
The centre is left empty to accentuate the

Coupe.

Claude-Nicolas Ledoux, *L'Atelier des Cercles*, 1804. Courtesy Bibliothèque Nationale de France

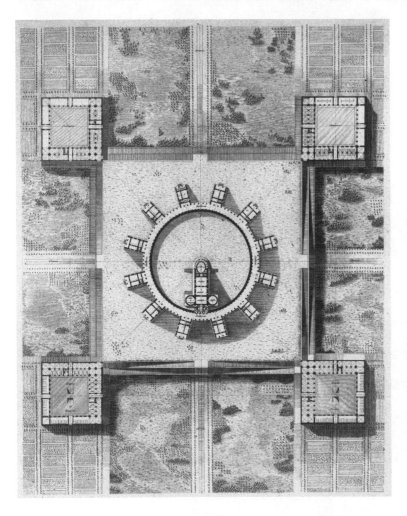

Claude-Nicolas Ledoux, *Maison des Gardes Agricoles*, 1804 bund *Maison de Plaisir*, 1780.
Courtesy Bibliothèque Nationale de France

Scientists and artists imagined globes so big that they became true architectural projects

mass of the cylindrical volume of the library. The supporting walls incorporate the bookshelves on three superimposed levels. For Boullée, architecture had a pedagogical scope. For him, the school of architecture is a school of reason and progress, where the new knowledge of nature and the history of mankind is presented in a dialectical way, from the origins of civilization to recent scientific discoveries. Here shines the genius of Newton.

GLOBES FOR AN IDEAL CITY

While Boullée articulated his utopian vision for the future of society through these large public monuments, his contemporary Claude Nicolas Ledoux (1736-1806) would use his architecture to build for all of humanity. As one of the favourite architects of the Ancien Régime, Ledoux worked with great success for the French aristocracy in the years preceding the Revolution. But after — or because of — the French Revolution, Boullée changed course radically, wanting to house the poor and claiming an ideal city for a new world. Ledoux's most important

project, the Royal Saltworks at Arc-et-Senans, is a complex dedicated to the salt industry. While Ledoux's first plan for the complex was a composition of buildings arranged around an immense square, linked to each other by porticoes, his second plan proposed a semi-circular complex that reflected a hierarchical organization of work, forming a perfect semi-circular plan reminiscent of the radiant sun. Although King Louis XV had approved of this second plan, only half of the complex was realized: the diameter and a semicircle of buildings for the saltworks.

After the (partial) completion of the project, Ledoux proposed to build an ideal city around the factory, called Chaux. The project — although never realized — testified to an architectural encyclopaedia where each function of society was characterized by a specific spatial form. Ledoux' catalogue of architectural elements was based on a series of geometrically pure forms (cube, sphere, cylinder, pyramid) that affirmed to a great extent his so-called *Architecture Parlante*, an architecture that overly states its function. The house of the water inspector, for example, is a large cylindrical volume embedded in a grand pedestal and incorporating both a river and a small waterfall. The barrel manufacturers' workshop, positioned at the crossroads of four routes, is another telling example. On the one hand, the square plan contains square rooms positioned at its four corners and a central fireplace; on the other, the elevation and section present a series of immense concentric circles surrounding a circular orifice. Gathered in space, the four wings form the intersection of two cylinders whose facades are decorated with concentric (perfect) circles that refer to the circles or hoops needed to secure the barrels for salt transportation. The house of pleasure is composed of twelve rooms coupled with baths for the pleasure of men and women, all attached to a perfect circular galleria. The entrance and the series of anti-chambers and salons are arranged in a phallic-shaped plan, leaving us in no doubt as to the complex's function.

If the aesthetics of the globe permeate many of the projects for this ideal city, it

Oscar Newman, *Plan for an Underground Nuclear Shelter*, 1969. Courtesy Kopper Newman

Richard Buckminster Fuller, *Biosphere*, Montréal, 1967. Photo D.C. Robidoux

is the housing for the agricultural guards, designed by Ledoux for Meaupertuis, that takes the most ideal form: a perfect sphere, embedded in a sunken rectangle, and accessible through a series of stairs positioned on all four sides.

THE GLOBE'S PHANTASMAGORIC POTENTIAL

French draftsman Jean-Jacques Lequeu (1757–1826) was inspired by the visionary models of Etienne-Louis Boullée and Claude-Nicolas Ledoux. His drawings, famous for breaking with every convention of symmetry, taste, proportion and artistic purity, testify to the concerns of his time. Lequeu proposed monumental public programmes, moralizing and reflecting a sublime ideal. This is what led Lequeu to enter, alongside Boullée and Ledoux, the circle of the so-called 'Architects of Liberty'. Composed of Gothic and classical motifs, his houses propose a profound profusion of symbols, especially phallic ones. Indeed, erotic and pornographic motifs were common in his drawings.[4] Lequeu was equally

inspired by the globe of the planet. His Temple for the Earth, conceived in 1794, is a perfect sphere enclosed by fourteen columns and set on a three-stepped pedestal with massive steps from all four sides. Dedicated to supreme wisdom, as indicated by the engraving on the entrance portal, this temple proposed a learning centre avant la lettre, where a circular seating area positioned under a vaulted stellar ceiling enabled those inside to study the globe positioned at its centre.

The utopian projects by Boullée, Ledoux (and Lequeu) have inspired more than one architect in the 20th century. In 1906, Samuel Friede announced his plan to build the Coney Island Globe Tower. This 210-metre-tall 'vertical theme-park' would contain Brooklyn's attractions in one giant globe in the air.[5] Had the plan gone through, the structure would have contained restaurants (one of which would rotate), an observatory, the United States Weather Observation Bureau and Wireless Telegraph Station, a vaudeville theatre, the world's largest ballroom, casinos, a hotel, a hippodrome, and a circus.

In 1967, Buckminster Fuller, together with Peter Chermayeff, Terry Rankine, Ivan Chermayeff and Shoji Sadao, proposed the Biosphere as the United States pavilion at the Montreal World Exhibition. Of all of Fuller's domes, the Biosphere is perhaps the most spectacular. Its 76-metre diameter and 62-metre height make it a dominating building on the St Helena Island. And although, geometrically, the dome is an icosahedron, a twenty-sided shape formed by the interspersion of pentagons into a hexagonal grid, it is substantially more spherical than any simple icosahedra. Its tubular steel structure is welded at the joints and thins gently towards the top so as to optimally distribute forces throughout the system. What Fuller imagined in all its utopian lightness, Oscar Newman imagined as a dystopian potential. In 1969, the American architect and city planner proposed a massive underground sphere beneath Manhattan. The hollowed space, cleared out with nuclear explosions, would house a regular city with a grid of streets and buildings, several levels of further underground spaces, and giant 'air filters' reaching the surface. Within a perfect sphere, housing, work and leisure would be organized under an artificially lit sky where coco-cola dances as a permanent cloud in the firmament.

In 1978, Rem Koolhaas added his own fascination for the globe to architectural history. In the appendix to his *Delirious New York*, he concludes his celebrated retroactive manifesto with the 'City of the Captive Globe' (1972). In this project, each 'island' corresponds to a city block and represents Koolhaas's theory of Manhattanism. The Captive Globe is suspended in the middle of the city, demonstrating that all ideologies contribute to the construction of the world, and nurture it; but equally that between the idea of the city and its reality, or, more precisely, between urban reality and its unconscious, there exists an inevitable gap.

Perfectly shaped, shimmering from all sides and holding an impeccable balance despite the laws of gravity, the sphere has been an object of fascination throughout architectural history: a means of tempting the gods in ancient Rome, the spatial articulation of the Enlightenment belief in the laws of nature, a key setting for an ideal civilization, or the protagonist of dystopian narratives. In each case, the sphere testifies to what Claude-Nicolas Ledoux wrote in 1804 in his *L'architecture considérée sous le rapport de l'art, des moeurs et de la legislation*: 'Architecture is to masonry what poetry is to literature; it is the dramatic enthusiasm of the profession; we can only talk about it with excitement.'[6]

1
Yann Rocher recently curated an exhibition entitled *Globes. Architecture and science map the world*, Cité de l'architecture et du patrimoine, Paris, November 2017–March 2018. See also the exhibition catalogue Yann Rocher (ed.), *Globes. Architecture et science explore le monde*, Paris: Norma Editions, 2017.

2
See, among others: Anthony Vidler, *The Writing of the World. Architecture and philosophie from Ledoux to Fourier*, Princeton: Princeton Architectural Press, 1987; *Les architectes de la Liberté 1789-1799*, Paris: Ecole Nationale Supérieure des Beaux-Arts, 1989.

3
He was a professor at the Ecole Nationale des Ponts et Chaussées from 1778 to 1788.

4
Lequeu offered his collection of more then 800 drawings in 1825 to the French National Library. Although some were considered pornographic or immoral and hence kept out of sight in the library's 'hell section', his drawings have safeguarded his important legacy over time.

5
Rem Koolhaas, *Delirious New York*, New York: Rizzoli, pp. 58–62.

6
Claude-Nicolas Ledoux, *L'architecture considérée sous le rapport de l'art, des moeurs et de la legislation*, Paris, 1804. Edition en facsimile, de Nobele editeur 1962. Larges extrait dans l'oeuvre et les rêves de Claude-Nicolas Ledoux, editions du Chênes, Paris, 1961.

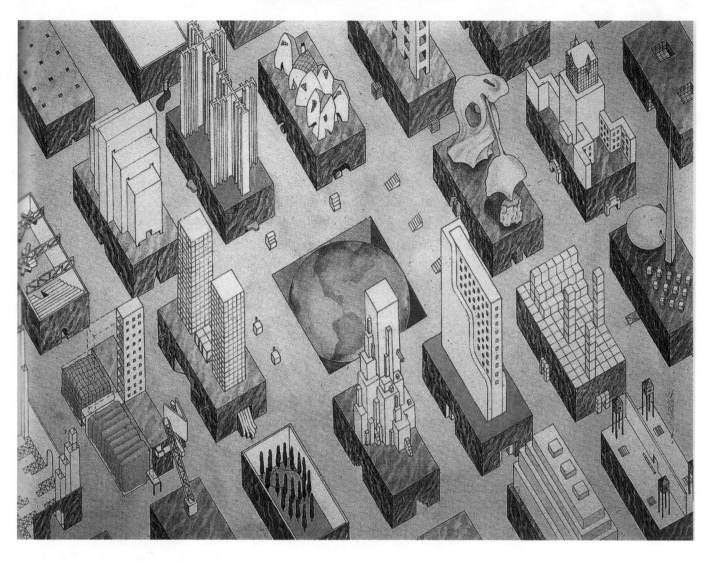

Rem Koolhaas, Zoe Zenghelis, Madelon Vriesendorp, *City of the Captive Globe*, 1972

POLPETTE

'I don't have a real recipe if that's what you want,' says my grandma, Catherine 'Rusty' Esposito down the phone from the East Coast. 'I can't say if it's a half a cup or three quarters of a cup, you know what I mean.'

I do. Italian-Americans are notorious for not measuring or timing when cooking. Mostly you grow up watching what's happening in the kitchen; you learn by feel and instinct. Trial and error. Sometimes, you just fake it. Sure, there are some necessary precautions when it comes to making pasta or biscotti, because that's dough territory. But with other things, you know when you know, you know? And nothing is more proof of this than in the making of the meatball.

Since the early 20th century no food besides pizza has been more representative of the Italian-American experience than that big garlicky multi-meat bulbous, usually found atop a big plate of pasta. Recall the date scene between Lady and the Tramp in the Walt Disney film: 'Now here you are, the best spaghetti in town,'

Tony says to the lovebirds, as they dive into a plate of spaghetti and meatballs in the alley outside Tony's Town Square Restaurant. When there's only one meatball left, Tramp rolls it across the plate to Lady, thus sealing the deal as Tony and his chef sing *Bella Notte* while playing the accordion and the lute. This is social class-defying romance courtesy of the aphrodisiac of stateside Italian cooking.

Or there's the seminal moment in *The Godfather* when the men are going to the mattresses (getting ready for the *famiglie* war, at their hideout apartment). Peter Clemenza shows Michael Corleone how he makes meatballs and red sauce: 'Hey come over here kid, learn something. You never know you might have to cook for twenty guys someday.'

Clemenza's meatballs and red sauce look similar to the dish I have always had when visiting my grandma in East Boston, which used to be an Italian-American enclave (now the population is mostly Central American). 'The real old-fashioned recipe for the meat part is you mix beef, pork and

Text by Ananda Pellerin

veal,' says 94-year-old Rusty, who still cooks them on the regular. 'And then I put in parsley — you can never have too much fresh, Italian flat leaf parsley; that makes them delicious. Garlic, three cloves at least. Grated Italian cheese, I use pecorino romano, they usually like parmesan but I don't like it, it has no flavour. Salt and pepper, bread-crumbs, but I don't use bread-crumbs, I use wet stale bread that I soak in either milk or water, then you squeeze out the water and you mix the bread in. And eggs.'

Like Clemenza, after browning off the meatballs she throws it in the 'gravy' (the Italian-American term for tomato sauce — one that some people are so attached to, you can buy a T-shirt that says, "It Ain't Sauce, It's Gravy!"). She also adds other types of meat including spare ribs or sausages — 'Pork makes the Italian gravy,' she'll tell you, 'I know that for a fact' (careful watchers of the prison cooking scene in *Goodfellas* will find affirmation of this) — and there it all cooks for about an hour until the whole shebang is served up on the table, to be scooped over pasta. 'I usually use rotini,' says Rusty. 'But you can use any kind of pasta you want. Ziti or wide noodles. I never use spaghetti, I hate it. I prefer linguini. Delicious.'

But the meatball is not just an Italian-American invention, it's a dish for the ages. If you find yourself at seriouseats.com, you might stumble across a gem called The International Meatball Index. From South Africa (skilpadjies) to Romania (chiftele) to Japan (tsukune), every culture has at some point seen fit to fashion an orb-shaped edible out of various ground meats. Serious eats indeed.

One of the upshots of the meatball's ubiquity is that its origins remain unknown. Through gospel to apocryphal tale to Wikipedia, history tells us that various versions of the meatball can be found as far back as Ancient Rome, the Qin Dynasty in China and in early Arabic cookery writings — though there is no way to prove how deep into the recess-es of human existence it really goes, or who's been talking to whom, or stealing recipes and

Lady and the Tramp, 1955. Courtesy Walt Disney

techniques from whom. A recent furore involved Sweden admitting on the country's national Twitter account that their world-famous ground beef meatball — two million of which are eaten each day at Ikeas around the globe — was invented in Turkey. 'Swedish meatballs are actually based on a recipe King Charles XII brought home from Turkey in the early 18th century. Let's stick to the facts!' the confessional tweet read.

While there is likely some truth to this — the traditional Turkish kofte is itself a type of meatball and most probably a precursor to the Swedish kötbulle — changing the nomenclature, as some people have suggested, seems unlikely, and perhaps unnecessary at this point. Sweden has come clean about the past, their meatball differs to the average kofte in texture and size, and every country can claim their own interpretation. Plus, who wants to break the heart of the Swedish Chef Muppet?

Like the dumpling, the meatball is a lowly yet lofty foodstuff that speaks directly to the human condition, finding expression across centuries and civilizations.

To say this is to say that the human condition has been, by and large, shaped by necessity. Meatballs and dumplings do not stem from the palace or ceremonial table (though fancy versions have of course found form). These are little parcels devised to feed large groups and make ingredients go far.

Over the centuries variations have appeared in response to shifting material conditions. Putting the disgraced Swedish kötbulle aside, the most famous meatball remains the super-sized version commonly found on the Italian-American table. The origin of this particular incarnation is the polpette, a small beef or veal round made in the old country, which is tiny in comparison to the whop-ping big balls you now get in the States. And as with most food in America, the story of the meatball is the story of class mobility. This particular chapter goes as such: of the four million Italians who immigrated to America between 1880 and 1920, 85 percent were poor folk from southern Italy, and they brought their food customs with them, including the polpette, served in tomato sauce. Once across the Atlantic, these new Americans found themselves having to spend less of their income on food. More money on food meant bigger balls. The Italian word for this experience of increased wealth is *abbondanza*, meaning 'abundance'; to live in plenty.

Following the verbal recipe handed down from her grandmother and then her mother, Rusty's meatballs are, and I say this without bias (...), consistently the best in the world. And while she isn't an enemy of change, she does caution against hubris. 'A lot of people put onions in their meatballs now,' she says. 'But I've never seen anybody that's a decent cook put onions in meatballs.' (Back to *Goodfellas*, the use of onions remains a point of contention.)

Of course it's not just Italian-Americans who have fallen in love with this version of the meatball. More than 49 million people have visited the over 28,000 Italian restaurants in the US in the last thirty days — and lord knows a good swathe of them have indulged in some S&M. The dish has travelled the world, too, even back to Italy, where it is — mostly likely begrudgingly — served at restaurants catering to the tourist trade. It's also made its way to more northern climes.

'The meatball is a classic for the British Italian family,' says Samantha Williams, executive chef of Cafe Murano and Murano in London. 'Albeit not authentically Italian, it has its place in the British homestead and dining scene. Through the years it has been served up with the classic spaghetti and meatballs. It's a favourite among the younger generation who dine in our cafés, with, dare I say... a sprinkle of parmesan.' (Close your ears Rusty...)

It's no mystery why meatballs have become so popular: they're delicious and, in theory, easy to make. What perhaps isn't as obvious is why meatballs are, well, ball-shaped. Some of it has to do with the shape of the human hand — it's intuitive to roll ground meat into an orb.

'I suppose a burger is flat to fit in a bun more easily,' says Williams. 'But in all honesty, I'm not too sure about meatballs. I suppose being round makes for a moist centre and it's a great shape for kids to stick a fork into.'

So, is the meatball round because it's fun? That's probably part of it. 'But you don't actually roll the balls,' Rusty is quick to point out, with a heavy note of caution in her heavily inflected Boston accent. 'Just drop them from hand to hand. Keep them light and not too dense.' Yet despite the meatball's inexplicable — and arguably artless — shape, it holds within its circumference countless stories of penury and new-found wealth, exploration and theft, Sunday dinners and evenings out. And behind it all, seasoned hands delicately rolling that world-shaped meaty mixture back and forth, back and forth.

Rusty preparing polpette.
Courtesy Ananda Pellerin

4.
THE LIFE
OF THINGS

Aldo van Eyck saw play as the way to rebel against the strait-jacket of modernism, while Rupprecht Geiger saw colour as an element and got high on red.

PLAYTIME

In the post-war decades, Aldo van Eyck filled hundreds of vacant city spaces with curves, circles and hemispheres, anticipating play as a provocation against the authoritarian architecture of modernism.

Text by Merijn Oudenampsen

In 1947, the architect Aldo van Eyck built his first playground in Amsterdam, on Bertelmanplein. Many hundreds more followed, in a spatial experiment that has positively marked the childhood of an entire generation. Though largely disappeared, defunct and forgotten today, these playgrounds represent one of the most emblematic of architectural interventions at a pivotal time: the shift from the top-down organization of space by modernist functionalist architects, towards a bottom-up architecture that literally aimed to give space to the imagination.

Immediately after the World War II, Dutch cities were in poor condition. The housing stock was falling dramatically short in both quantitative and qualitative terms. Combined with a dysfunctional infrastructure, it presented planners with an outright emergency. On top of that, this ravaged urban landscape was soon confronted with a peak in birth rates, later referred to as the post-war baby boom. That despite the almost total lack of space for children, inside and outside the home. Some playgrounds did exist in the city at the time, but almost all of them were private and open exclusively to the fortunate few as members. Van Eyck's playgrounds, initially built on temporarily unused plots of land, can be seen as an emergency measure, but they had a significance far beyond that of a creative solution at a time of need.

THE FUNCTIONALIST CITY

Post-war urban planning in the Netherlands mainly consisted of the hasty and economized implementation of the pre-war ideals of the modernist movement grouped around the Congrès Internationaux d'Architecture Moderne (CIAM), identified with the work of modernist architects like Le Corbusier, Giedion and Gropius. In Amsterdam, Cornelis van Eesteren, long-time president of the CIAM, was to implement his General Extension Plan (AUP) of 1934, one the first modern urban master plans based on extensive statistical forecasts of demographic and transport developments.[1] His plan embraced the ideal of functional separation, meaning that housing, work, traffic and recreation were to be functionally separated and inte-

grally planned. This was the basic premise of the large-scale construction of new post-war neighbourhoods in the 1950s, such as Buitenveldert and the Western Garden Cities, resulting in the familiar open housing blocks with large amounts of light, air, greenery and monotony.

But the agenda of functional separation also resulted in the conclusion that Amsterdam's economic centre needed to expand and the old city had to be 'opened up' to traffic. This vision was radicalized in the 1960s when the entire city clogged up due to the explosive rise in car traffic. Urban planners introduced a proposal for an extensive network of metro lines and highways to cut through the old fabric of the city. What was on the agenda was a tabula rasa makeover of Amsterdam's 19th-century ring of popular and dilapidated neighbourhoods: the Jordaan, Nieuwmarkt, Eastern Islands, Weesperbuurt and Pijp.[2] A wholesale urban modernization wave that would form a 20th-century version of the hitherto unrealized 19th-century Hausmannization of Amsterdam, much like Robert Moses famously used 'the meat-axe' to make space for his parkways and causeways in New York. The Dutch planners, however, never got that far. They were soon to encounter a huge protest movement in their way that effectively threw sand in the machine, and finally defeated what was by then called the 'urban bulldozer'.[3] Aldo van Eyck played an important role in defining what would follow.

1.
Vincent van Rossum (1993) *Het Algemeen Uitbreidingsplan van Amsterdam: geschiedenis en ontwerp*. NAi publishers, Rotterdam.

2.
Gemeente Amsterdam (1968) *Voorontwerp tweede nota over de binnenstad*. City of Amsterdam.

3.
Bergh & Keers (1981) 'De Binnenstad als Vrijetijdscentrum'. In: *Wonen TA/BK*, no. 19, October 1981, pp. 2–18.

BREAK WITH FUNCTIONALISM

Van Eyck's path and that of the functional modernist school were initially one and the same. When he started on the playgrounds, Aldo van Eyck worked directly under Cornelis van Eesteren, who was in charge of Amsterdam's urban development department until 1959. He also began to participate actively in the CIAM conferences. However, the perspective on urban space that Van Eyck developed through his playgrounds, would lead him to become one of the most fervent critics of the functionalist tendency that dominated the CIAM movement until then. 'Functionalism has killed creativity,' Van Eyck stated in an article in the Dutch magazine *Forum*. 'It leads to a cold technocracy, in which the human aspect is forgotten. A building is more than the sum of its functions; architecture has to facilitate human activity and promote social interaction.'[4]

Between 1947 and 1978, Van Eyck designed hundreds of playgrounds, first for the Department of Urban Design and later on (in 1952) for the municipality, working for his own office. In the first eight years, he designed sixty of them, and after that many more, the last ones almost in batches in the new post-war districts. Of the grand total of seven hundred, only ninety survived into the 21st century with their original layout. The first playground on Bertelmanplein was a test case. Van Eyck designed a sandpit bordered by a wide rim. In it he placed four round stones and a structure of tumbling bars. The pit was placed in the north corner of the square, diagonally across from three tumbling bars. Bordering the square were trees and five benches. The playground was a success. Many designs followed and, depending on the site, Van Eyck deployed a number of compositional techniques.

For him the playgrounds were an opportunity to test out his ideas on architecture, relativity and imagination. Relativity in the sense that connections between elements were determined by their mutual relationships rather than by a central hierarchical ordering principle. All elements were equal: the playgrounds designed by Van Eyck were exercises in non-hierarchical composition.[5]

Van Eyck also designed the playground equipment himself, including the tumbling bars, chutes and hemispheric jungle gyms, and his children tested them. To him, play equipment was an integral part of the commission. The purpose was to stimulate the minds of children. The hemispherical jungle gym was not just something to climb. It was a place to talk and a lookout post. Covered with a rug, it became a hut. These sandpits, tumbling bars and stepping stones were placed throughout the Netherlands.

Different elements of the playgrounds represented a break with the past. First and foremost, the playgrounds proposed a different conception of space. Van Eyck consciously designed the equipment in a very minimalist way, to stimulate the imagination of users (the children), the idea being that they could appropriate the space by its openness to interpretation. The second aspect is the modular character of the playgrounds. The basic elements — sandpits, tumbling bars, stepping stones, chutes and hemispheric jungle gyms — could endlessly be recombined in differing polycentric compositions depending on the requirements of the local environment. The third aspect was the relationship with the urban environment, the 'in-between' or 'interstitial' nature of the playgrounds. The design of the playgrounds was aimed at interaction with the surrounding urban tissue. The temporary character of the intervention was part of this 'in between' nature, recreating space through incremental adaptation instead of the tabula rasa approach of modernism, in which the designs had an autonomy of their own, based on abstract data and statistics. Of course the use of empty plots was also a tactical solution. Because the Site Preparation Service of the Department of City Development, working together with

4.
Aldo van Eyck (1959) 'Het Verhaal van een Andere Gedachte' (The Story of Another Thought). In: *Forum* 7/1959, Amsterdam and Hilversum.

5.
Lianne Lefaivre & Ingeborg de Roode, eds. (2002) *Aldo van Eyck: Playgrounds*. NAi Publishers, Rotterdam.

local associations, wanted to give every neighbourhood its own playground, they often had to be placed on vacant, unused sites.

THE PLAYGROUND
AS CULTURAL CRITIQUE

The playgrounds were not isolated architectural interventions. Somehow, they served as a powerful synthesis, a distillation of some of the most interesting motives that resonated amongst the last avant-gardes in that interesting timespan when modernism came under heavy fire, but the general disillusionment of the post-modernist era was nowhere yet in sight. In itself, a playground seems a rather sweet and non-controversial undertaking, but at the time, it also functioned as a crystallization point of cultural critique.

In 1949, Van Eyck played host to the first exhibition of the Cobra group — a short-lived but influential avant-garde art movement — at the Stedelijk Museum in Amsterdam. The Cobra group drew inspiration in particular from children's drawings. They believed that the spontaneity of children's imagination, untainted by modern protocol, was one of the privileged sites of authenticity in a society where man was to live 'in a morbid atmosphere of artificiality, lies and barrenness'.[6] The close relationship between Van Eyck and the artists from the Cobra current makes it probable that much of his early inspiration for the playgrounds derived from Cobra: 'On the margins of attention there is always the artist, essential companion to the child. His function is too decorative,' Aldo van Eyck stated during CIAM X in Dubrovnic in 1956.[7] The Cobra group dissolved only three years after it was founded, but Cobra members Constant Nieuwenhuys and Asger Jorn were to reappear on the stage as co-founders of the Situationist International in 1958.

In that context, the notion of play also gained symbolic importance. In 1938, the Dutch historian Johan Huizinga wrote *Homo Ludens*, a book on the historical importance of the element of play in culture[8]; Constant Nieuwenhuys used the idea as the basis for his critique on urbanism. Much like Aldo van Eyck, he was

deeply critical of the functionalist architecture of the post-war period. Together with Guy Debord, he drafted the now famous tract on *Unitary Urbanism*, which proclaimed the advent of a society of mass creativity. Due to mechanization, Constant proposed, Homo Faber, the traditional working man of industrial society, would be replaced by Homo Ludens, the playful man, or creative man, in post-industrial society.[9] The Situationists took this element of play and developed it into one of their core notions, as Debord would state: 'Due to its marginal existence in relation to the oppressive reality of work, play is often regarded as fictitious. But the work of the situationists is precisely the preparation of ludic possibilities to come.'[10] The situationists, whose ideas came to play an important role in the 1968 rebellion, developed the notion of play into a subversive strategy to rebel against modern capitalism and modernist architecture; Le Corbusier's authoritarian architecture was portrayed as a form of fascism. With psychogeography and the famous *dérive*, they changed focus from 'streets, buildings and businesses' to how 'people inhabit the city and the collective psychic ambiances they project', much

6.
Cobra #4, 1949, cited in W. Stokvis (1980) *Cobra. Geschiedenis, voorspel en betekenis van een beweging in de kunst van na de tweede wereldoorlog*. De Bezige Bij, Amsterdam.

7.
Aldo van Eyck, 1959.

8.
Johan Huizinga (1952/1938) *Homo Ludens. Proeve eener bepaling van het spelelement der cultuur*. Tjeenk Willink, Haarlem.

9.
Mark Wigley, ed. (1998), *Constant's New Babylon: The Hyper-Architecture of Desire*, 010 Publishers, Rotterdam.

10.
Guy Debord (1958) Contribution to Situationist Definition of Play, Internationale Situationniste #1, June 1958, Paris.

in parallel with Van Eyck's stress on place and occasion.

After leaving the situationists, Constant was to play a role in the Dutch spirit of 1968. In his famous utopian work of architecture *New Babylon* (Van Eyck actually assisted him when he started making scale models), Constant created an explicit metaphor for the advent of a creative society. He saw his ideas on mass creativity materialized in the youth culture of the 1960s, where his ideas were taken up by the Dutch yippies, the provos, that through playfulness and endless provocation brought the authoritarian spirit of the Dutch 1950s down on its knees.[11]

END BATTLE

In the Netherlands, modernist urban planning and the growing anti-modernist spirit of revolt were to have a final confrontation in the Nieuwmarkt neighbourhood in Amsterdam. This was the site where the first of the metro lines — with a four-lane inner-city highway on top — was to be constructed, cutting through one of the oldest popular neighbourhoods of the city. Hundreds of students, artists and activists moved into the empty buildings of the neighbourhood, where provos together with a mix of residents and activists founded *Aktiegroep Nieuwmarkt*. Years of spirited resistance, and a conclusive violent riot in 1975, led to the final surrender of the modernist planners and the politicians who headed them: the metro line was built but the highway was abandoned, and all other metro plans were off the agenda.

The New Left came to power and the Nieuwmarkt was saved, to become an inspiration for anti-modernization struggles elsewhere in the country. A new model for urban development emerged — 'building for the neighbourhood' — that replaced large-scale modernist interventions with small scale participative projects in the neighbourhoods. The 'structuralist' architectural philosophy of Aldo van Eyck and the group around *Forum* magazine was to become a template for a decade to come. One of the first and most symbolic of these projects was the redevelopment of the Nieuwmarkt itself. Maybe not so surpris-

ingly, Aldo van Eyck was the architect to work on it. Here, his ideas on interstitial space, non-hierarchical composition, and participative planning led to an architecture that could easily mould into the existing tissue of the neighbourhood. 'Play,' as Huizinga once said, 'is a serious matter.'

Constant Nieuwenhuys, *New Babylon* (Ruimtecircus), 1956. Photomontage Jan Versnel. Courtesy Fondation Constant

11.
Richard Kempton (2007) *Provo: Amsterdam's Anarchist Revolt.* Autonomedia, New York.

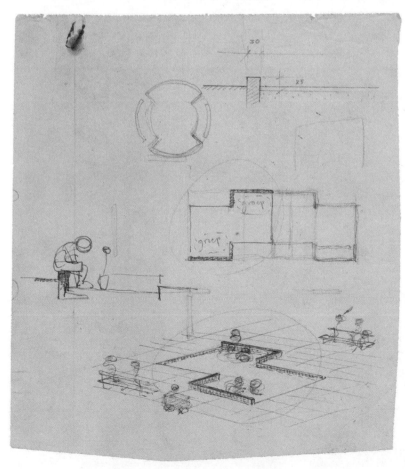

Drawings of Bertelmanplein playground, Amsterdam, 1947. Courtesy The Aldo van Eyck Archive. Opposite page: Bertelmanplein playground, Amsterdam, 1947. Photo City of Amsterdam. Courtesy The Aldo van Eyck Archive

Child in the Snow

You all know what happens after a heavy snowstorm? The Child takes over — he is temporarily Lord of the City. You see him darting in every direction collecting snow off frozen automobiles. A great trick of the skies, this, a temporary correction for the benefit of the neglected child. It is up to you now to conceive of something for the child more permanent than snow — if less abundant, something quite unlike snow in that it provokes movement without impeding other essential kinds of urban movement.

It must be conceived furthermore not as an isolated thing or isolated set of things, but as something which can be repeated on suitable places in the city. The city must be able to absorb it both aesthetically and physically; it must become part of the city's everyday fabric.

It must be elementary in that it must respond to the child's elementary inclinations and movements (the latter does not completely cover the former) and activate his imagination.
— Aldo van Eyck, 1969

From the *The Child and the City*, a project set in 1969 by Aldo van Eyck for architecture students at the Harvard University Graduate School of Design, USA.

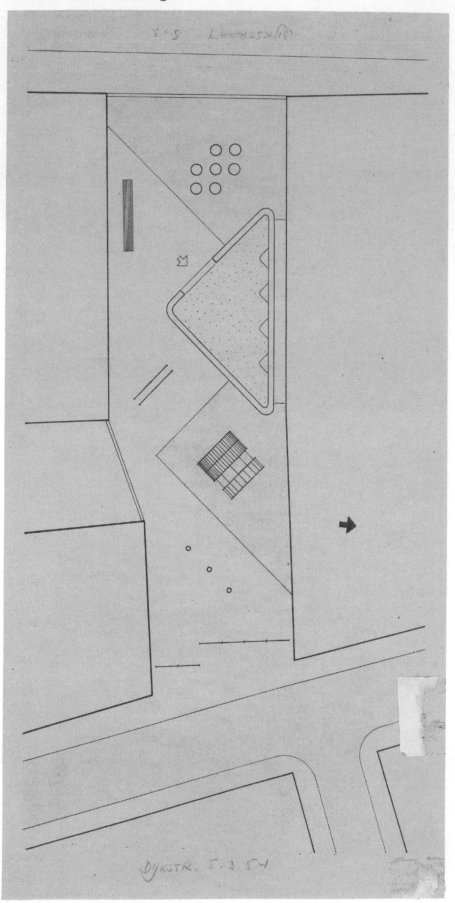

Drawing of Dijkstraat playground, Amsterdam, 1954. Courtesy The Aldo van Eyck Archive. Opposite page: Dijkstraat playground, Amsterdam, 1954. Photo City of Amsterdam. Courtesy The Aldo van Eyck Archive

THE BALL HAS NOT YET REACHED THE GROUND

The first person to hang upside down from the flip bars of the playgrounds designed by Aldo van Eyck was often his daughter Tess, an experience she vividly remembers to this day.

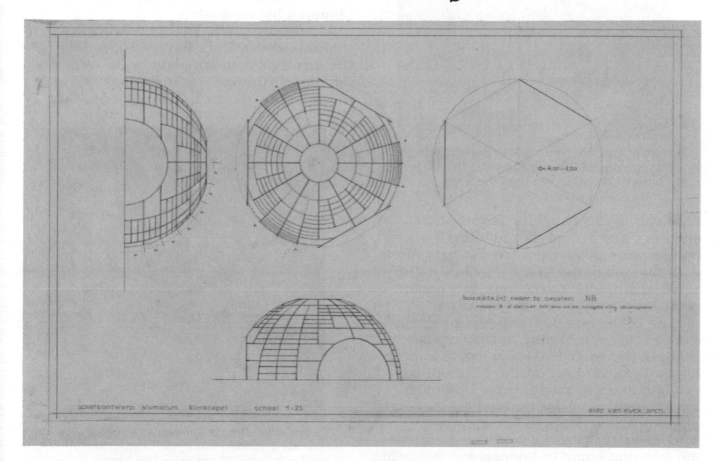

Text by Ernst van der Hoeven

Aluminium climbing domes, flip bars and concrete sand pits: in the post-war years generations of Dutch children grew up in playgrounds by architect Aldo van Eyck (1918–1999). He designed over seven hundred iconic public play areas of which —according to the latest count — only seventeen are left. They occupy a firm place in the collective memory of the Dutch — ask any baby boomer at random about their childhood, and Van Eyck's climbing igloo is sure to feature — and indeed in architectural history, in which Van Eyck's anti-functionalism caused a stir as recently as the 1980s. 'Functionalism has killed creativity,' he declared in an article in the Dutch magazine *Forum*. 'It leads to a cold technocracy, in which the human aspect is forgotten. A building is more than the sum of its functions; architecture needs to facilitate human activity and promote social interaction.'

Hannie and Tess van Eyck at Bertelmanplein playground, 1947. Photo Aldo van Eyck. Courtesy The Aldo van Eyck Archive

Aldo van Eyck's daughter Tess is also an architect, and one of those children who hung upside down from the flip bars. Along with the rest of the Van Eyck family, she acted as a model for the very first photographs of Van Eyck's playgrounds. In a picture of the one on the Bertelmanplein, she can be seen playing in the concrete sandpit. Her mother Hannie sits in a winter hat and elegant coat on the edge of the sandpit, like a character from a different era. Suddenly you realize how astonishingly modern that sandpit was.

I meet Tess van Eyck in the garden of her parental home in Loenen aan de Vecht, a garden that became famous in the 1970s because of a meeting of TEAM 10, a group of architects that split off from the Congrès Internationaux d'Architecture Moderne (CIAM) in the second half of the twentieth century and left its mark on the architectural debate with its ideas about the 'functional city'. I recognize the garden from a 1974 photograph of the TEAM 10, a circle of informally dressed men, and the occasional woman, on a lawn. There was no money to rent a different location, and the folding chairs were fetched from the studio. Tess van Eyck describes how her father studied architecture in Zurich before the war and came into contact there with Sigfried Giedion and Cornelis van Eesteren, the secretary-general and chair of CIAM respectively. 'When Aldo returned to the Netherlands after the war, Van Eesteren immediately gave him a job in the Reconstruction Department in Amsterdam. Van Eesteren had large-scale, visionary plans for the city. He proposed demolishing much of the historic city centre. The scale and impact of the plans would have been colossal. Aldo was utterly opposed and tendered his resignation.'

Ironically, it was Van Eesteren who then introduced Van Eyck to Ko Mulder, one of the first female urban planners to work for the city of Amsterdam. She was employed in the Public Works Department and had

Team 10 meeting in the back garden of Hannie and Aldo van Eyck, Loenen aan de Vecht, 1974. Photo Peter Smithson. Courtesy The Aldo van Eyck Archive

Previous pages: Aldo van Eyck on the roof of Amsterdam Municipal Orphanage, 1960. Photo J.J. van der Meyden. Courtesy The Aldo van Eyck Archive

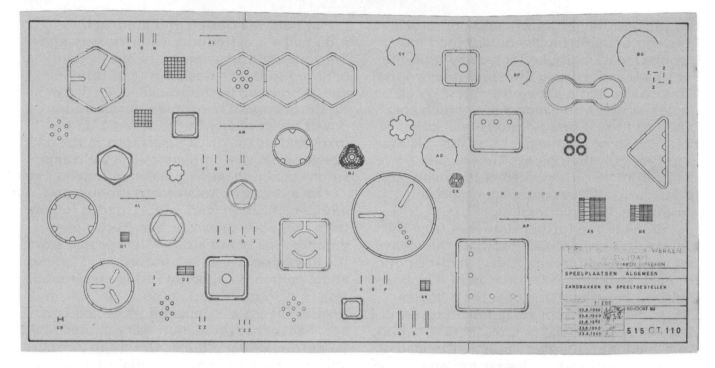

Drawing of sandpits, somersault frames, climbing frames, play tables and climbing mountains, 1960.
Courtesy The Aldo van Eyck Archive

passionate ideas about increasing the number of play areas in the city. In those days playgrounds were surrounded by fences. Mulder aspired to create open play areas that were better integrated into the city. The first task she gave Van Eyck was to design a playground for the Bertelmanplein, an existing square in south Amsterdam. In the archives, Tess van Eyck shows me some sketches of the Bertelmanplein. 'These are the very first drawings that indicate how Aldo saw the relationship between playing children and playground equipment. In his design the emphasis was on the child's imagination, without any specific use being laid down. For that reason he disliked slides and swings. Hanging, climbing and jumping all involved exploring the human body in relation to the elemental. To illustrate his concept of relativity, the idea that all viewpoints are equivalent and that there is no centre, Aldo liked to quote a line from a poem by Dylan Thomas: 'The ball I threw while playing in the park has not yet reached the ground.'

Shortly after the war, Van Eyck watched his own children growing up on the Binnenkant in Amsterdam, a bustling inland harbour with improvised play areas. 'As children we played a lot on the street and on the quaysides,' Tess van Eyck remembers. 'The harbour district was full of crates and tea chests we could jump onto, and we clambered onto the railings next to the steps to the front doors of the houses.

What I still remember vividly is the great sensation of hanging upside down from those bars.' His children's remarks caused Van Eyck not just to make space for the imagination but to regard that imagination as gender neutral. 'He wasn't interested in the role-playing as play today, but in the child playfully exploring, discovering, inventing, imagining.' Van Eyck's first playground on the Bertelmanplein, a sober design with a sandpit, some flip bars and a couple of arched climbing frames, was a huge success from the start. Local residents, and people from other neighbourhoods, urged the council to provide more. Slowly but surely, Van Eyck's play areas spread out like an oil slick across the city. The Van Eyck family tried them all out: 'When more playgrounds were built, we went with my mother from one to the next. None of them had precisely the same equipment, which was something we really loved about them.' Unusually for the climate of post-war reconstruction, in which efficiency was all, Van Eyck's play areas were always site specific. The relationship with the surrounding buildings and open spaces between housing blocks determined the layout. Occasionally he took away from the car (road) and gave to the child (playground). There was often a geometric interplay of circles, squares and rectangles, which combined to form a three-dimensional composition. The important aspect was the relationship between the objects. He wanted children to go on a voyage of discovery and to be 'enticed' from one play object to another by their placement.'

Showing me further drawings from the archive, Tess van Eyck describes the ideas behind the equipment. 'Aldo's starting point for each structure was the way in which children move and discover their bodies. Often, they start with small challenges and then move on to bigger ones, daring to jump from higher and higher spots — the idea of distance, relationship, dimension and shape, all those things that children learn through play.' The sandpit with the wide concrete sides was there from the beginning, and the rest developed over the years. 'The arch came before the climbing dome, and the first arch on the Bertelmanplein was smaller. In the 1960s the big concrete stepping stones were introduced, then the concrete climbing hill, like the one in the playground in the Vondelpark that's still in use.' Rubber paving, football fences and helmets had yet to arrive. 'Today everything is so 'overprotected'. Children have completely lost their freedom of movement in cities. They used to be able to play on the street. There were completely different ideas about safety and rules, but it didn't lead to more accidents. I recently heard that there was only one really serious incident in a Van Eyck playground. That was because the child was wearing a helmet and got stuck between the bars because of it.'

Tess van Eyck shows me a map of Amsterdam with all the play areas built between 1947 and 1978. Different colours convey information about the part played by Aldo van Eyck who, during the last years acted more as a supervisor and less as a designer. She recalls how at first someone from Public Works would come to the Binnenkant every time a playground was built. 'He'd have a map with nothing on it. Then Aldo would create a design.

In both his design and approach, Aldo had a great affinity with the way non-Western cultures express themselves, as opposed to the Cartesian way of thinking and expressing in the so-called 'civilized' Western world. The primary forms and power of simplicity he discovered on his many travels to Africa resurfaced in his own design work, also in his playground compositions concrete, paving slabs and metal bars.

As a result of Amsterdam's renovation and densification, and new attitudes to play, from the 1980s onwards, Van Eyck's playgrounds slowly but surely disappeared from the cityscape. There is now renewed interest and a certain revaluation of his playgrounds from a cultural-historical point of view, and several have been declared protected heritage. 'Sadly, that protection has not prevented them from being altered. Often the paving stones, which form an essential part of the composition, have been replaced with rubber tiles. Other elements were removed too,' Tess tells me. 'I hope they can one day be used again in their original form. The playgrounds are so elemental and urban in a contemporary sense. Local councils and developers concern themselves with public space, but that usually means a square with cafés, some tables outside, a few trees. You wonder what the children are supposed to do while their parents sit on a bistro terrace.' I suggest they'll probably look at their phones. Tess responds with laughter: 'Yes, you do have to work really hard to distract them from those. But it really is necessary. Children are getting fatter all the time. The ball has not yet reached the ground.'

GEIGER AT THE KUNSTAKADEMIE DÜSSELDORF, 1974. PHOTO DIETMAR SCHNEIDER

A LIFE IN SPHERES

Absorbed by the setting sun over Chiemsee lake, Rupprecht Geiger survived the horrors of war and devoted his life to painting portraits of colour, especially at the red end of the spectrum.

Text by Kirsten Algera and Ernst van der Hoeven

Photos courtesy Archiv Geiger

If you look at paintings by architect and artist Rupprecht
Geiger (1908–2009) and close your eyes, the after-image will
remain on your retina for several minutes. It's just like looking
at the sun with your eyes shut. And that is precisely the inten-
tion, Geiger says. 'To really see colour, you must close your
eyes and imagine it,' he writes in his 1975 book *Farbe ist
Element* (Colour is Element). It would be an understatement
to describe Geiger's works as 'Colour Studies'. They look too
radioactive for that, his oeuvre too radical. Practically all his
works include the same freestanding 'spheres' in a colour that
sweeps you away. Again and again, in painting after painting,
silk-screen print after silk-screen print and installation
after installation, Geiger attempts to show pure colour. It is as
if he wants to free the colour from form and from its context,
initially blue and yellow, then from the 1970s onwards the
entire red spectrum, from orange to carmine and from
magenta to vermillion.

 Geiger's former studio stands in a wild garden on the
southern edge of Munich. It has now been turned into an
archive and opened to the public. As you walk through it,
Geiger's obsession with colour becomes tangible; even the
washbasin next to the toilet is covered in fluorescent paint.
Geiger carried on painting until the very last day of his
101-year life, by his own account 'High on Red'. Granddaughter
Julia Geiger, who assisted him in his later years, tells us
about his work in the studio where Geiger's brushes and
pigments still lie as they did in the moments after he last
used them.

Julia Geiger and Franziska Straubinger in the Geiger Archive, 2018. Photo Taufiq Hosen

It's astounding how you have preserved all of this for almost ten years now. It feels as though it were only yesterday that Rupprecht Geiger was here.

> This was precisely our intention. We wanted to capture the atmosphere of him working here. I think it allows us to see his art in a different way than, for instance, in a 'white cube'. Many people are extremely enthusiastic about seeing where his art was made and can even understand the creative process better after visiting the studio. That's why we wanted to change as little as possible. We still refuse to have the paintings that belong to the archive framed behind glass. The works can only be properly perceived without an unnecessary barrier.

How would you describe your grandfather's work?

> He wanted to create a portrait of colour. By all possible means. For seventy years he worked constantly and consistently on this topic. And he was quite resourceful in creating the portrait of colour. He always tried new things, be it in the application of paint, in his use of binders, or even in the idea of how to convey colour itself to the beholder. It wasn't only paintings or silkscreens; he also created accessible colour tanks and rooms. Or he incorporated dead, amorphous material and placed it alongside colour. It was his intention to find ways to enhance the perception of colour.

Did the colour red play a role in his personal life?

> He collected everything red. At one point I even stopped wearing red scarves or jewellery because he would always ask whether he could have them, to include them in his collages for example. It was a kind of game for him. When people came to visit, they'd often try and dress inspired by my grandfather's colours. He loved that and would collect these objects, such as red buttons. The colour red fascinated him.

Did he share his fascination with his family?

> I once had an unforgettable experience as a child at the Chiemsee. My family has owned an old farmhouse there since the 1930s, and of course I was there quite a bit during my childhood. The Chiemsee is a large lake in Bavaria, and we always went to the same restaurant by the shore to have dinner and also to watch the sunset. I remember well how Rupprecht was absorbed by this. As children we weren't allowed to make a sound then. 'Be silent,' he'd say. 'And watch.' And during these ten minutes, when the red ball would sink into the lake, we'd be still and just watch. I remember how he himself would gleam in a bright red from the rays of the setting sun.

His work really was a part of his life then.

> Rupprecht actually did live with his art. One of his paintings from the 1970s hung above the sofa in his living room for many

years, and he liked to have his picture taken in front of it. It's
a glowing orange 'pressed' circle. And of course he went to his
studio on a daily basis to work there. He never skipped a day.
Even on the day of his 100th birthday! We'd organized a little
party in his home next door, but after a while he left and went
to his studio.

Your grandfather was a trained architect. How did he become a painter?

Rupprecht studied architecture, and his father Willi was a
painter and graphic artist, quite known in his day. I think my
grandfather chose to be an architect in order to distance himself from his father's occupation. On the other hand, his father
taught him everything he knew about art. Rupprecht was in
fact an autodidact when it comes to drawing and painting. The
crucial time that showed him he ought to pursue painting was
the war. He was sent to Russia and was in charge of telephone
and train connections in Wjasma near Moscow in 1941/42. This
is where he made his first watercolour drawings and kept a
diary where he'd sketch and write down his thoughts. Later on
he said he needed this form of distraction for therapeutic use,
in order to deal with the cruelty the war had unleashed.

Russian War Diary, 1941, 21 × 31 cm (opened), Archiv Geiger

He was allowed to make art on the battlefront?

He painted three works in total during that time. His father,
who originally had been listed as a 'degenerated artist', took
these paintings to the Ministry of War and was able to have
Rupprecht appointed a war painter. So Rupprecht then had the
task of portraying generals in the Ukraine and Greece and
to depict German victories in a heroic manner. However, as of
1942 Germany no longer had victories, and Rupprecht then
focused on the Mediterranean atmosphere when he arrived
in Greece in 1944. There are beautiful diary entries where he
writes about how he is fascinated by the bright light and
intense colours. He drew cityscapes and landscapes in gouache
or watercolour.

589/70 (WV 566), acrylic on canvas, 270×290 cm, 1970. Photo Andreas Pauly

Zweimal Rot/leuchtrot kalt auf rot-orange (WVG 109-1), silkscreen, 1968. Photo Bogdan Braikov

From *Rupprecht Geiger – Eight Silkscreens* (WVG 129-3), silkscreen, 1970. Photo Bogdan Braikov

rot-orange auf leuchtrot kalt mit Spritzer auf weiß (WVG 108-2), silkscreen, 1968. Photo Bogdan Braikov

So the war made him an artist.

> Yes, you could say that. The war was an integral experience.
> Later on he'd say that the years of war were the years of his
> autodidactic study of painting. After World War II he couldn't
> immediately get back to work as an architect. However, he
> continued to work as one from 1947 after the currency reform
> until the early 1960s in order to support his family financially.
> Up until then he hadn't been able to live off his paintings.
> His heart, however, did beat for painting.

Is there any work left from this period?

> Rupprecht had the order to depict German victories. And so
> he had to present what he had made. When the clerk saw the
> paintings from the Ukraine and Greece, he said no German
> would know what to do with them. That's why my grandfather
> was allowed to keep the paintings. And we are fortunate to
> have most of these early paintings in the archive since many
> works by German war photographers and artists are still in
> American archives.

Did he experiment with colour in his war years?

> In a way he did. The first three landscapes he made during the
> war depict parts of a barren landscape. When you cover the
> bottom half of it you can see the modulation of colour in the
> sky. This technique of creating a colour gradient surfaced again
> and again in his works up until the last painting.

It's fascinating that he decided to be a radical abstract artist from an early time on. In 1949
he already started working with concepts the ZERO group would use ten years later in
Düsseldorf.

> Rupprecht's works during and shortly after the war were in fact
> figurative; there is still a reference to the real world. After the
> war many artists, not just Rupprecht, were in search of an
> adequate style, an adequate language. Some artists decided to
> return to the old, while others decided to move in the opposite
> direction. The idea of the artist group ZEN 49 — Rupprecht
> being one of the founders — was to spread abstract art by
> means of paintings and by word. Rupprecht repeatedly wrote
> that one could no longer depict the real world after having
> experienced such cruelty during the war.

So his colour studies started just after the war.

> During the years of 1948/49, Rupprecht started working on
> so-called 'shaped canvases', in which the composition dictated
> the frame. This experiment with form and frame paradoxically
> led him to focusing on colour itself. However, Rupprecht felt
> this group of works was too daring. He didn't show the works
> to anybody, not even his closest friends. And so they lay forgot-
> ten in a corner of his father's studio, where Rupprecht was

permitted to paint once a week. Only after his father's death in the 1970s did he rediscover them. They influenced his colour field paintings of the 1970s; he started focusing on the colour red and archetypal shapes like the rectangle and the 'pressed' sphere.

Is there a connection between his move to the Rhineland and these shapes?

I think that it reflects a development within Rupprecht's oeuvre. He gradually stepped away from reality. He started using fluorescent pigments that do not exist in nature and are chemically produced. His goal was for his works to evoke as few associations as possible; that's why he numbered his works. If you have an archetypal shape such as an oval or even a monochromatic colour field, you only focus on the colour itself. Düsseldorf does in fact stand for a new chapter in terms of vocabulary of shapes, drawing utensils, and application of paint. From this moment on he only worked with fluorescent pigments; before then he only used them sparingly within his works.

They were industrially used pigments?

Exactly. They were developed in the 1940s in the USA for military purposes, for marking roadways and missiles. Then advertising quickly discovered them, and Rupprecht was the first German artist who used these pigments within the fine arts.

He made his own paint?

Yes. He added a binder to the industrial pigments that he bought by the barrel; egg until 1955 and later oil. However, oil does 'swallow' a lot of the colour's intensity, so he started using an acrylic binder as of 1965, the year of his move to Düsseldorf. Acrylic paints can be processed quickly, they dry rapidly and the pigments' brightness is hardly affected. In Düsseldorf he also started working with an industrial airbrush. He didn't want any recognizable brushstrokes to be seen. No handwriting, so the colour can speak for itself. Rupprecht wanted to 'disappear' behind the colour.

How did he create the monumental colour fields? We saw a photograph of a painting lying on the floor...

The picture base had to lie flat or else the colour would trickle while he was working with the airbrush. However, it is a mystery to us how he worked on the really large paintings from that time in that technique. With smaller formats he simply worked with stencils. He always primed his canvases with a white colour. During the 1960s he used silverscreens a few times that were ready-to-use. After using the airbrush he went back to using paint rollers and regular paintbrushes, working on the canvases vertically again. Rupprecht always first applied the lightest colour and gradually made the colour darker by adding more pigments. That's how the gradient of colour took shape.

That must've been physically quite straining if you can't interrupt the process.

Yes. It was especially so with the large-scale works for a Sao Paolo exhibition, which he made when he was 94 years old. We even designed a special chair for him then that could be adjusted in height, allowing him to work from the top down. He worked about four to six hours per colour field. After, he couldn't work for about a week, he needed a break to recharge. And I feel this energy in turn comes back to the beholder of his works.

Geiger with assistant working on *Transatlantic*, for XXV Bienal Sao Paolo. Photo Julia Geiger

It sounds like he was looking for a way to leave the war behind him for his entire life.

Maybe. He did talk about his war experiences frequently. As he got older, many experiences resurfaced. At breakfast he would tell us about the nightmares he had from the war. However, at the same time these experiences were the initial impulse for his art. Rupprecht often described the observation that occurred shortly after the war in the grey ruins of the Promenadenplatz in Munich. Piles of rubble surrounded him when he saw a young girl wearing a magenta-coloured cardigan get out of a Jeep. And while she walked away she left a bright coloured trail behind her. This instant is what my grandfather called the *Farberlebnis* — the colour experience. Inspired by this encounter, he created the painting *E 190a*.

In a catalogue we read it was made with lipstick.

That's right. Originally it was drawn with a bright pink lipstick that he had received in a care-package. Hilla von Rebay, director of the Guggenheim Museum in New York at the time, had asked the Moderne Galerie directors Otto und Etta Stangl whether certain artists and art historians could be supported in the American Zone, Rupprecht thus being one of them. He received a care-package with coffee, painting utensils, and a pink lipstick which was actually meant for my grandmother. This once-pink trace on the painting has faded over time. On the back you can still see the greasy residue from the lipstick. The colour experience in the ruins of war was so important to my grandfather that he made a panel in the early 1970s on which he described this occurrence and traced the girl's trail again, this time in fluorescent pigments.

It's fascinating how his works look so contemporary. Do you notice an increasing interest in his work because of this?

It could well be that his work didn't receive the appreciation that it could've obtained had he painted them today. In fact, for a series of posters for a concert series in Munich during the 1960s he had to tone down the colour. The authorities thought that the bright colour would distract drivers on the road. Nowadays these colours don't shock us anymore. During the 1960s, however, many people shook their heads while walking through a Geiger exhibition and seeing these fluorescent pigments. Rupprecht composed a text in which he stated: 'Why am I not an American? If I were an American I'd receive international recognition, which I don't have in Germany.' In Munich he also waited a long time in vain for a professorship before going to the Rhineland. Only upon his return in the 1980s did he start receiving any kind of appreciation for his work.

In his installations he enhanced the effect of colour by also colouring the ceiling and the floor. How did he get from paintings to environments?

Rupprecht was an architect and you can certainly sense that within his art. There are three-dimensional works in his oeuvre that unfold within space. He was looking for a way to set colour free from outer factors that compromise the perception of colour itself. This is when he developed the idea of colour tanks. He made his first colour tank for an exhibition at the Folkwang Museum in Essen in 1975. The walls and ceiling were painted red and fluorescent tubes lit up the space. Visitors were to actually meditate in this room and to refuel on colour and energy. One idea that unfortunately wasn't executed was to have the inside of an old Gasometer in the Rhineland painted in pink or red. In an interview with Hans Ulrich Obrist for his 100th birthday, Rupprecht stated that he would love to set up large colour tanks in all big cities so people could experience colour and refuel on energy during their lunch breaks. He wrote: 'Red is a drug. Red is life, energy, potency.' He was high on red until the end.

Rupprecht Geiger's Studio, 2018. Photo Taufiq Hosen

Barrels filled with fluorescent pigments. Photo Taufiq Hosen

Rupprecht Geiger's sink, 2018. Photo Taufiq Hosen

5.
APPENDIX

A TRANSIT OF VENUS happens when the sun, Venus and Earth are in perfect alignment. From Earth, you can observe a small black disc — Venus — slowly crossing in front of the sun over the course of several hours. This happens in a pattern that repeats every 243 years: there's a gap of 122 years, then a pair of transits spaced eight years apart, then a gap of 105 years, then another pair. The most recent transits occurred on 8 June 2004 and 6 June 2012. Those who witnessed the 2004 transit were the only human beings then alive to have ever seen it. One of them was photographer Wolfgang Tillmans. *Venus Transit* (page 209) and *Venus Transit, Drop*, 2004

PHOTO COURTESY ADAM ŠTĚCH

LA MADRE, il Figlio e l'Architetto (The Mother, the Son and the Architect) is a short film about a church in the form of a sphere in Gibellina, a town in Sicily that was destroyed by an earthquake in 1968 and replaced by a new town in the 1980s. Filmmaker Petra Noordkamp came across the church by chance and was intrigued by its remarkable design. The narrator in the film, her alter ego, says: 'For me, visiting a building is like watching a film. Roaming through the corridors is choreographed by the architect who decides where you turn a corner, who predetermines the window through which you can lose yourself in a view…' Her fascination with the building intensified when she discovered that the church was designed by the influential Italian architect Ludovico Quaroni (1911–1987). He was the father of Emilio Quaroni, a young man with whom Noordkamp had had a brief romance in the 1990s. After losing contact with Emilio for some years, in 2001 she discovered that he had murdered his own mother in the same year that they had a brief relationship. The film ruminates of what made Emilio commit such an act and explores how her perception of the architecture is affected by an encounter some fifteen years earlier.

Balls (2018), Lernert & Sander

Artist duo Lernert & Sander transformed 98 golf balls into meticulous cubes of 25 × 25 mm. *Balls* is available as C-print, 400 × 318 mm, in an edition of 50, printed on Ilford Goldfiber Silk, signed by the artists. Price €500 excluding framing and shipping.

www.macguffinmagazine.com/shop

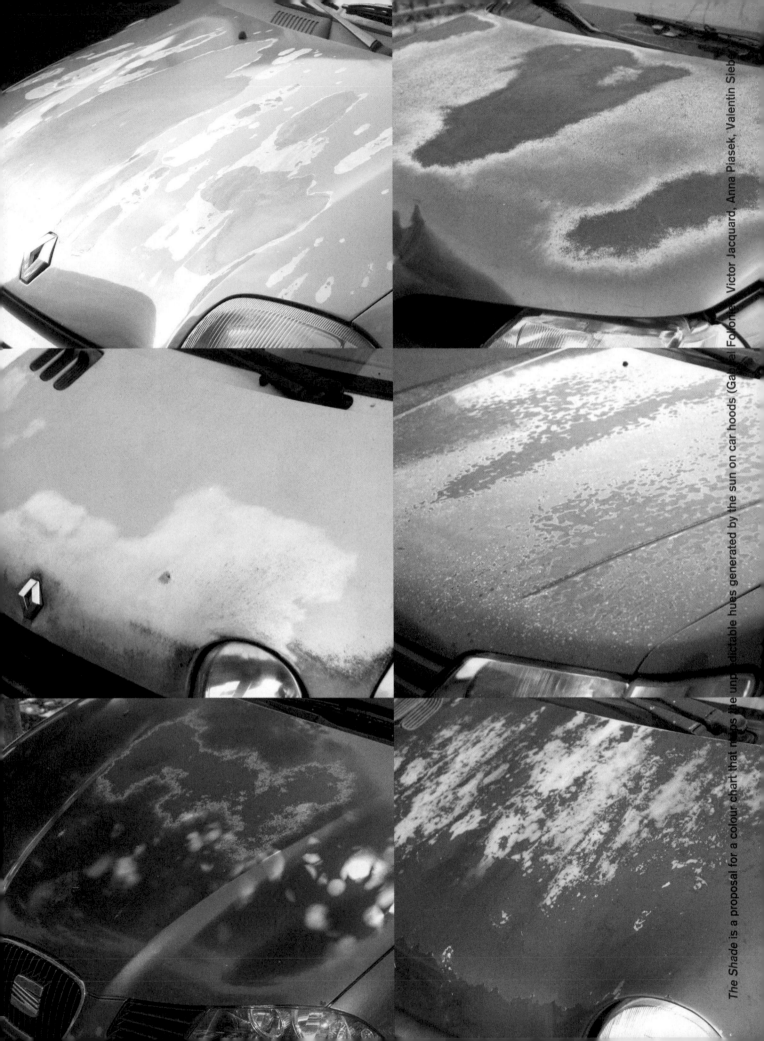

The Shade is a proposal for a colour chart that maps the unpredictable hues generated by the sun on car hoods (Gabriel Fontana, Victor Jacquard, Anna Piasek, Valentin Siebe...

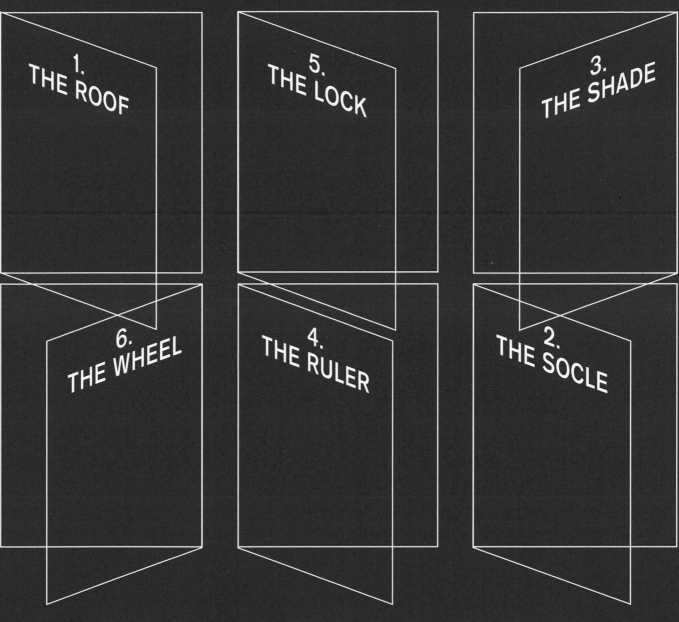

1.
THE ROOF

5.
THE LOCK

3.
THE SHADE

6.
THE WHEEL

4.
THE RULER

2.
THE SOCLE

ECAL X MACGUFFIN

Can a magazine be a design school? Or a design school a magazine? This autumn, MacGuffin and Swiss art and design school ECAL present the results of their collaboration during the 4th Istanbul Design Biennial, which is all about design as learning, and learning as design. The exhibition explores the ways in which the two can enrich the other.

Last autumn, Dutch product designer Chris Kabel tutored undergraduate students at ECAL in collaboration with design magazine MacGuffin. The students used the magazine's editorial model as a methodology to study the use of everyday things and to design objects derived from them.

They modelled their approach on the way the magazine themes its issues, and chose MacGuffins like The Roof, The Shade, The Wheel, The Ruler, The Lock and The Socle as the focus of their investigations.

Their research resulted in a range of observational studies, contextual reportages and visual essays on the materiality of the objects, to be used as a basis for designing new objects. The outcome is an exciting collection of narratives and objects that explore *The Life of Things*, presented in the form of a 3D magazine. From Umbrella Stories and Wheel Stoppers to Real-Life Rulers and a platform for the Bottom of Things.

The Life of Things, Istanbul Design Biennial – A School of Schools, curated by Jan Boelen. Pera Museum, Meşrutiyet Caddesi 65, İstanbul. 22 September – 4 November 2018. www.aschoolofschools.iksv.org

LEWIS M. RUTHERFURD, THE MOON, ALBUMIN PRINT, 1865. COURTESY SCIENCE PHOTO

Lawyer and astronomer Lewis Morris Rutherfurd (1816–1892) was a practically minded scientist, much interested in instruments and their usage. He built new gadgets himself or had them made under his supervision. With the help of his friend and telescope manufacturer Henry Fitz, he developed the first photographic telescope. Unprecedented photographs of the moon, sun and stars were taken in Rutherfurd's private observatory in his New York garden. The picture from 6 March 1865 is regarded as the best photograph of the twelve-day-old moon.

'Football is War' has headed the lists of sporting clichés for decades. American writer Don DeLillo devoted a fascinating book to it during the Vietnam War, called *Endzone* (1972). The central character, Gary Harkness, a football-playing student, becomes increasingly obsessed with the idea that football and war are one and the same. One of his teachers tries to shake him awake: 'I reject the notion of football as warfare. Warfare is warfare. We don't need substitutes because we've got the real thing.' Perhaps football isn't always war, but war is sometimes football. Even in ancient times, sport and warfare were closely linked. Pantarces of Elis, having won the Olympic horse racing in 365 BCE, went on to lead the peace talks between the Achaeans and the Eleans. In spite of the modern Olympic charter, which states that politics must not enter the Olympic arena in any form, the relationship between balls and bombs is profound in the modern age too.

BALLS AND BOMBS

Text by Kirsten Algera

01

CHRISTMAS BALLS, 1914

In November 1914 it became clear that the First World War would not, as initially thought, be over by Christmas. On the contrary, both the Germans and the Allies were digging in more than ever. In defiance of warnings from the British high command, soldiers began swapping cigarettes, in protest and out of boredom. On Christmas Eve 1914 the Germans struck up 'Stille Nacht',

ending with a message shouted in English: 'Tomorrow is Christmas; if you don't fight, we won't.' Before long the next morning, footballs were being fired at the other side instead of bullets and shells. The football games went on into January 1915. Not everyone was pleased. A corporal by the name of Adolf Hitler, serving close to Ypres, demanded that football be forbidden. His advice was taken up by British general Sir Horace Smith-Dorrien, who reminded his men that 'Friendly inter-course with the enemy is absolutely prohibited.'

02

BLOOD IN THE WATER, 1956

On 6 December 1956 the Cold War reached a climax in the Olympic pool in Melbourne. A few weeks earlier, the USSR had crushed the Hungarian revolt in the streets of Budapest, and the mood of the water polo match between the Hungarian and Soviet teams was less than friendly. Furthermore, most of the audience was made up of Hungarian immigrants and Australians and Americans stirred up by Cold War rhetoric. We do not know what was said in the pool, but Russian-speaking Hungarians had come prepared for a game of Soviet-bashing. 'We'd decided to try to make the Russians angry to distract them,' Hungarian captain Ervin Zádor said later. They certainly succeeded. There was a great deal of thumping and kicking, as the Hungarians drew 4-0 ahead. In the final minutes of the match, Zádor was marking Soviet player Valentin Prokopov, with whom he had already exchanged words. Prokopov struck him, causing a bleeding gash. Zádor left the pool and the sight of his blood was the final straw for a crowd already in a frenzy. Angry spectators jumped onto the concourse beside the water and threatened the Russians. Police entered the arena and shepherded the crowd away. After the match, Zádor and some of his gold-medal teammates sought asylum in the West.

03

SOCCER WAR, 1969

The only war that has actually acquired the name of a ball game, the Soccer War, lasted only 100 hours, but it claimed thousands of lives. Immigration problems and land reforms had caused rising tensions between Honduras and El Salvador over a number of years. The qualification round for the 1970 FIFA World Cup lit the fuse. During the first match, on 8 June 1969 in Tegucigalpa, Honduras, riots broke out between the supporters. At the second match on 15 June 1969 in the capital of El Salvador, violence inside and outside the stadium could not be contained. An unknown number of Salvadorans in Honduras were killed or injured, and tens of thousands began fleeing the country. A week later El Salvador broke off diplomatic relations with Honduras. This did not, incidentally, prevent a victory by the Salvadorian team in the third qualifying match, which they won 3-2 in extra time. In the belligerent climate stirred up by the press, the El Salvadorian army invaded Honduras on 14 July. Honduras called on the Organization of American States to mediate and on 20 July a ceasefire was announced. In 1970 El Salvador travelled to the World Cup in Mexico, where it ended bottom of its group.

04

PING-PONG DIPLOMACY, 1971

Not Mao or Richard Nixon but Glenn Cowan and Zhuang Zedong, two table-tennis players, were responsible for the 1971 rapprochement between China and the United States, countries that had not been on speaking terms since 1949. It all started when Cowan, a member of the American table-tennis team, missed the American bus during the 1971 World Championships in Japan. He was given a lift by the Chinese team and got talking with Zhuang Zedong, a hero in his own country, through an interpreter. Zedong said to Cowan, 'Although the US government is unfriendly to China, the American people are friends of the Chinese. I give you this [silk print] to mark the friendship from Chinese people to the American people.' The Chinese team then invited their American counterparts on an all-expenses-paid trip to China, which would include a few rounds of table tennis. 'The Ping Heard Round the World,' was the headline in *Time Magazine*. Although the American team lost to its hosts, the result was that China allowed more foreign journalists into the country and the United States lifted its twenty-year embargo on trade with China. So at last the stage was set for the first state visit to China by an American president, in 1972. The repeated offer by Cowan to chair the talks between the Chinese premier Zou Enlai and Richard Nixon was not taken up. His pilot for a television programme on ping-pong led nowhere either. He was admitted to a mental institution and died in 2004. Zedong was arrested in 1976 and spent four years in a Chinese rural prison camp. He devoted the final years of his life to calligraphy.

05

THE HAND OF GOD, 1986

The stories told by Argentine footballer Maradona are not always consistent. Take his handball against England in the quarter finals of the World Cup in Mexico in 1986. At the press conference after the match, Maradona explained that he had scored the goal 'un poco con la cabeza de Maradona y otro poco con la mano de Dios' (a little with the head of Maradona and a little with the hand of God). Years later he took God out of the equation and said he had used his hand to score as revenge for the defeat of Argentina in the Falklands War. 'This was our revenge, it was ... recovering a part of the Malvinas. We all said beforehand that we shouldn't mix the two things but that was a lie. A lie! We didn't think of anything except that; like hell it was going to be just another game!' The Hand of God had meanwhile gone on to lead a life of its own. It inspired the founding of the 'Church of Maradona,' a branch of the Catholic Church with 80,000 disciples, where the ball is central and an alternative Our Father has been composed: 'Our Diego, who is on the pitches, Hallowed be thy left foot, bring us your magic. Make your goals remembered on earth as in heaven. Give us some magic every day, forgive the English squad, as we have forgiven the Napolitan Mafia. Don't let yourself get caught offside and free us from Havelange and Pelé. Diego.'

06

GADDAFI HOCKEY

In 1987 the West German ice hockey club ECD Iserlohn was on the verge of bankruptcy. Owner Heinz Weifenbach had an innovative idea: a sponsorship deal with the Libyan dictator Muammar Gaddafi. 'Heinzy' was a wayward bon vivant who would wave a pistol in the dressing room if he felt the team had performed poorly. That tough attitude may have won him the respect of the team, but it left the tax authorities, which were owed €3.4 million by ECD Iserlohn, cold. When they refused to be fobbed off any longer, Weifenbach flew to Libya along with the mayor of Iserlohn and persuaded Gaddafi to pay €900,000 for the next season. In return, the team would advertise Gaddafi's Green Book — a collection of the dictator's political philosophy and other ramblings — on their shirts. The team was delighted when Weifenbach returned with the money, but the German government and the ice hockey association were not amused. In the previous year a bomb attack on a Berlin disco had been blamed on Libya and the US had bombed Tripoli in retaliation. 'What at first looked like a carnival joke is a flagrant violation of the political neutrality of the sport,' said the German minister of internal affairs. Weifenbach thought the commotion ridiculous. He argued that his club was simply advertising a book, which happed to have been written by Colonel Gaddafi. 'I thought the era of book-burning was over,' he said. At the next EDC Iserlohn match, in Frankfurt, the riot police had to protect the team from an angry crowd. In the dressing room a proposal was put to the vote: continue being paid and wear the shirt with the Green Book, or carry on in the old shirts unpaid. The players made the best of a bad job and Weifenbach wound up the club. Gaddafi is said to have decided to put his money into weapons for the IRA the next time.

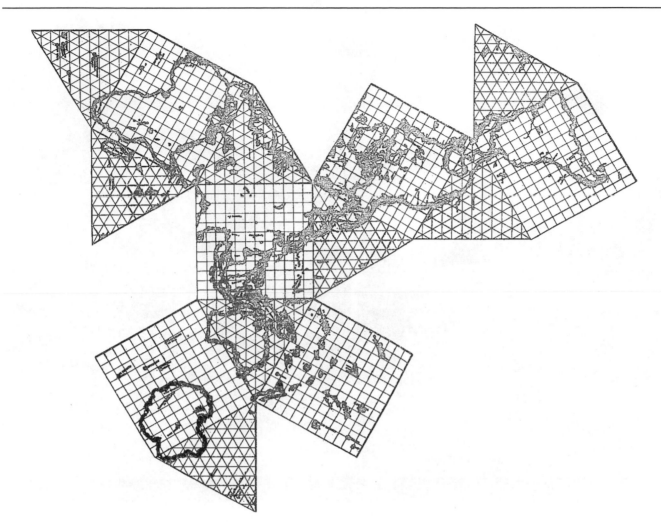

DYMAXION MAP, R. BUCKMINSTER FULLER, 1944

1.   FROM ROUND TO FLAT AND BACK AGAIN

Since time immemorial, people have been trying to make a flat map of the spherical earth, in such a way that all the continents are shown and the mutual proportions are correct. For example, Leonardo da Vinci chopped the globe in two halves and flattened each hemisphere with four cuts, making his world map look like two mounted butterflies. Hendrik Mercator is the most influential mapmaker. The sixteenth-century Fleming was the first to use a conformal map projection, which served as the standard for centuries, but also gave a distorted image of the world. The countries near the equator appear very small compared to the giant landmasses at higher latitudes.

Countless cartographers have devised new projections in every imaginable form, from hanging potato peels and pentagrams to recumbent Ts. In 1943, a battle was waged in the *New York Times* between supporters of Bernard Cahill's Butterfly Map and the tangram-like Dysmaxion Map by R. Buckminster Fuller. Two wonderful projections that are loved by cartophiles but which never made it into an atlas, because Mercator remained the norm. Much to the annoyance of German historian Arno Peters, who presented a controversial map of his own in 1975.

Opponents spoke of a distorting mirror, of continents that were 'hung on the polar circle like wet laundry'. The Peters projection map, with a marginal Europe, was adopted by development organizations and the quest for the ideal world projection continued.

In 1988, the hundred-year-old National Geographic Society held a competition for the best representation of the spherical shape on a flat surface. Arthur Robinson won. Ten million *National Geographic Magazine* subscribers received a copy of the world map and the Robinson projection was adopted by hundreds of newspapers and magazines.

In the context of 'decolonization' the Peters projection has become topical again. But the most politically correct representation of our planet remains the globe. In the whole world, there are two studios where these are made by hand. One of them is Bellerby & Co. Globemakers in London. The studio began in 2008 when Peter Bellerby struggled to find a quality globe for his father's 80th birthday present. He decided to make his own. After two years of trying, he figured out how to create the perfect globe.

www.bellerbyglobemakers.co.uk

2.   BULB HOUSES

In a suburb of the Dutch mediaeval town of Den Bosch lies a field containing fifty globe-shaped houses. These futuristic-looking white *bolwoningen* (which translates as 'bulb houses') were designed in the late 1970s and — thanks to a Dutch fund for experimental architecture — realized in the same year (1984) as the celebrated 'cube dwellings' by Piet Blom in Rotterdam. The concrete cylinder on which they stand contains a staircase that rises to the living space where six round windows, a large rooflight and an absence of room dividers suggest more space than the actual 55 square metres these bulb houses offer.

Their architect, the artist and sculptor Dries Kreijkamp (1937–2014), was a great fan of the globe shape because 'it combines the biggest possible volume with the smallest possible surface area. So you need minimum material for it. It's space saving, very ecological and nearly maintenance-free.'

Kreijkamp knew what he was talking about. He lived in a prototype bulb-house complex consisting of two-and-a-half globes placed on the ground. The houses in Den Bosch should have been built according to this model, but due to building regulations and a fear of the unknown, Dreijkamp had to make several changes: one bulb per house, placed on a stalk and made of cement instead of polyester.

Despite these compromises, the houses attracted attention from all over the world. While Kreijkamp was dreaming of mass production, the first cracks and leakages appeared and the housing association considered demolition. In the end they were saved, but when the architect offered to build a few more the city replied: 'We already have some, thank you very much.'

Shocked by this ignorance but fuelled by optimism, Dreijkamp worked on the evolution of his creation until his death. He designed floating versions with an outboard motor and even found a Dubai factory that could produce the polyester balls. 'For 102,000 euros you get a maintenance-free sustainable house, including flooring, bathroom and beds. What more could you want?'

---

3.   BLIZ-AARD BALL SALE

PHOTO DAWOUD BEY. COURTESY JACK TILTON GALLERY

One winter morning in 1983, David Hammons set up a stall on the corner of Cooper Square in Lower Manhattan. He carefully arranged his merchandise on a colourful rug. What he was about to sell were snowballs. They looked as though they were produced by a machine and varied in size from XL to XS. By the end of the day he had sold the lot. For a dollar a piece.

Hammons' unannounced street action went down in art history as the *Bliz-aard Ball Sale*. The only

traces left of this celebrated performance are some oral accounts and a few photographs made by American photographer Dawoud Bey. On these pictures we see Hammons with hat, sunglasses, scruffy coat and dirty shoes standing behind his rug or offering an XS snowball to a child in a stroller. Looking and acting just like any other street vendor, the artist becomes invisible.

You could easily see *Bliz-aard Ball Sale* as a humble comment on

the art-world craze and on the poverty of many New York citizens. Besides that, it is just a very poetic and witty work by a conceptual artist (inspired by Arte Povera) who is known for making himself difficult to find — fusing art with life and vice versa. In Hammons's notion of an artist, words like illicit and fraudulent appear. And indeed, what could be more of a scam than selling snowballs in winter?

4.　　SILVER DORODANGO

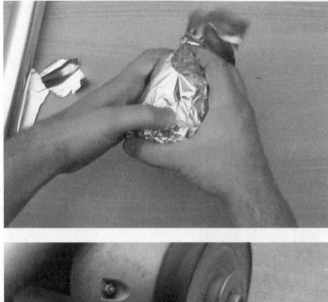

The latest Japanese ball craze is making a shiny ball of aluminium foil. YouTube offers lots of instructional material. First you form a sphere. Then you hammer all the wrinkles out of the foil. After that, you grind and polish the ball till it shines like a mirror. Once finished, there's not much you can do with it.

This online trend of 2018 is very similar to a Japanese ball boom of twenty years ago, called *hikaru dorodango* (a ball of mud that shines). To make such a ball you need dirt, water, and lots of patience. Which lots of Japanese must have, because all over the country people were hooked on making shiny mud balls.

Education professor Fumio Kayo came across the DIY phenomenon at a nursery school in Kyoto, where he saw young children absorbed in shaping a sphere

and putting all their energy into polishing the ball until it shined. It offered him fresh insight into how play helps children's growth. To facilitate further observations, he developed a time-consuming, shiny-mud-ball-making method that could be performed by even the smallest children.

While teaching, Kayo noticed that two-year-olds imitated everything he does, three-year-olds snatch his dirt, and older children are too proud to participate. Some children share information about where to find the best dirt, while others deliberately keep this information to themselves. But in the end, they all treasure their self-made dorodango as the most precious thing on earth. For all this, Kayo found the very essence of child's play in a 1990s ball craze.

5.   FALL OF THE WRECKING BALL

It is unclear who invented the wrecking ball, but it became the industry standard in the 1940s and was widely used for the next two decades. The technology behind the demolition device is rather elemental. A massive ball of forged steel weighing as much as 5,500 kilograms is hung from a crane and swung into a building, letting inertia and gravity do the majority of the work.

This basic technique proved to be an incredible innovation. Prior to the use of the wrecking ball, most buildings were taken down by teams of workers known as 'barmen', who would 'deconstruct' a building brick by brick. A giant metal ball could do the job much faster and cheaper.

In the 1960s the dirty and noisy demolition practice had to adapt to stricter regulations. It was not just the ever more sensitive environmental concerns that contributed to the fall of the wrecking ball. In the latter half of the 20th century hydraulic excavators arrived on the demolition scene. These new machines could nibble away at buildings in a very controlled fashion. And explosions or implosions could take down large structures even faster than wrecking balls.

Demolition today is transitioning back to a trend of deconstruction. Though wood may be reclaimed and concrete recycled, the wrecking ball still remains the quintessential symbol of demolition, probably because of its romantic associations. There's even some poetry to it (and several songs written about it). In its heyday — during the 1950s and 1960s — demolition was associated with progress and optimism. Wrecking balls were getting rid of the old and making way for the future.

WRECKING BALL DEMOLISHING THE BEISSER LUMBER COMPANY BUILDING, 2006

DEATH BY BALLS

VISUAL STORY BY:
ENZO PÉRÈS-LABOURDETTE

AS A SEVEN-YEAR OLD I REGULARLY LISTENED TO THE AUDIOBOOK BEWARE OF THE GRONK.
THE GRONK IS A BALL-SHAPED TOY WITH A MANUAL. IN THE BOOK, A BOY FINDS THE BALL BUT
DOESN'T READ THE MANUAL. WHEN HE PLAYS WITH THE BALL IT APPEARS TO BREATHE AND
GROWS LARGER AND LARGER. THE BOY USES THE LARGE BALL TO SIT ON, BUT IT STARTS HUNTING
HIM. ONCE READ, THE INSTRUCTIONS BECOME PAINFULLY CLEAR: 'DON'T SIT ON THE GRONK, OR IT
WILL SIT ON YOU.' SO I DECIDED TO STAY AWAY FROM BALLS.

BALLS CONTINUED TO CLAIM VICTIMS AT HIGH SCHOOL. MY VERY FIRST CLASS WAS PHYSICAL
EDUCATION. WE HAD TO ASSIST ONE ANOTHER WHILE WALKING ON BALANCING BALLS. THE BOY I

MY REFUSAL TO PLAY WITH BALLS RESULTED IN A COMPLETE INABILITY TO CATCH THEM WITH ANY OTHER PART BODY THAN MY FACE. I HAVE VIVID MEMORIES OF WET, MUDDY AND SANDY BALLS HITTING ME SQUARE ON THE NOSE.

PARTNERED UP WITH CLIMBED ONTO A BALL AND REFUSED TO HOLD MY HAND FOR BALANCE, CLAIMING ONLY GAYS HOLD HANDS. HE FELL OFF AND BROKE HIS ARM.

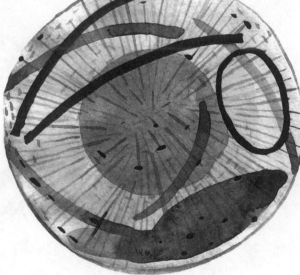

02.

03.

01.

04.

05.

BALLS ARE A DANGER
TO ALL. MY DECISION AS
A CHILD TO STAY AWAY
FROM THEM SAVED ME
FROM TERRIBLE FATES I
LEARNED ABOUT IN THE
NEWS:

27 - 02 - 2018
03. QUEENSTOWN, NEW ZEALAND.
WHILE PLAYING GOLF WITH
FRIENDS, A PLAYER IS STRUCK
ON THE HEAD BY A GOLF
BALL AND DIES.

25 - 02 - 2016
01. WISCONSIN, USA.
A MAN FIRES BOWLING BALLS
FROM A CANON IN HIS
BACK YARD. ONE OF THE
BALLS CRASHES INTO A
NEIGHBOUR'S BARN AND KILLS
A HORSE.

11 - 08 - 2008
06. ADÉ, FRANCE.
A PÉTANQUE PLAYER DIES
AFTER HE LOOKS TOO CLOSELY AT
THE PIGLET (A SMALL WOODEN
BALL THAT THE BALLS ARE AIMED
AT) AND IS ACCIDENTALY HIT BY
A PÉTANQUE BALL FROM A
FELLOW PLAYER.

10 - 01 - 2013
02. DOMBAI, RUSSIA.
TWO TOURISTS PAY FOR
A ROLL IN A ZORBING BALL.
(A LARGE INFLATABLE BALL IN
WHICH YOU CAN ROLL DOWNHILL)
THE BALLS VEER OFF COURSE. ONE
OF THE MEN DIES AFTER THE BALL
DISAPPEAR OVER THE EDGE OF A
CLIFF.

15 - 10 - 1983
05. NEW YORK CITY, USA.
AT THE US OPEN AN ERRANT
TENNIS BALL HITS A LINESMAN
IN HIS GROIN. HE FALLS
BACKWARDS OFF HIS CHAIR
AND DIES FROM THE
IMPACT TO HIS HEAD.

06.

07.

08.

09.

10.

11.

18-06-09
10. LAS VEGAS, USA.
A LION DIES AFTER EATING A
RUBBER AMERICAN FOOTBALL.
THRIFT STORE EMPLOYEES WORKING
NEXT TO THE ZOO HAD LEFT
THE BALL OUTSIDE THE FENCE.

31-10-01
07. SANDY, UK.
A MAN FEELS NUMB AFTER BEING
HIT ON THE NECK DURING A GAME
OF PAINT-BALL. HE DIES IN BED
OF A STROKE CAUSED BY THE
IMPACT OF THE BALL.

28-02-2005
08. ABERDEENSHIRE, UK.
A 10-YEAR OLD BOY DIES AFTER
A GIANT SNOWBALL WEIGHING
NEARLY HALF A TON ENGULFS
HIM WHILE ROLLING DOWN
A HILL.

23-10-2009
09. MONTREAL, CANADA.
A WRECKING BALL ACCIDENTALLY
DETACHES FROM IT'S CHAIN
AND LANDS ON TOP OF A
METALWORKER WORKING
NEARBY.

17-04-1959
10. KARACHI, PAKISTAN.
A YOUNG CRICKET PLAYER
IS HIT ON THE CHEST BY
A BALL. HE DIES FROM
CARDIAC ARREST.

14-07-11
11. CLEVELAND, USA
AN EXOTIC PET OWNER IS FOUND
DEAD IN HIS BEDROOM, HAVING
ACCIDENTALLY CHOKED ON A
BALL-GAG WHILE MASTURBATING.

Yearly MacGuffin
subscription:
37€ EU — 42€ WW

Visit: www.macguffin
magazine.com/shop

KIRSTEN ALGERA
is an Amsterdam-based editor, writer, curator and lover of all sports without a ball. As a child, she was rushed to the doctor with a marble stuck in her nose.

CHRISTINE BJERKE
is an architect and educator based in Copenhagen. She experienced the immense power of the ball at the Chichu Art Museum in Japan. A large black ball by artist Walter De Maria reflected the bare concrete space by architect Tadao Ando. The simplicity of the shape and its reflections of the surrounding space questioned nothing and everything at the same time.

MEREL BOERS
is a historian, writer, argumentation specialist and bouncy ball. A playground marble champion at age seven, but don't put her in goal in any ball game.

POL ESTEVE
is an architect, teacher, researcher and co-founder of the architecture studio GOIGOIGOIG. As an architecture student, he realized that architecture was made not only of columns, but also of disco balls.

TESS VAN EYCK WICKHAM
is an architect with projects in the UK and the Netherlands. In recent years she has spent more and more time working on the Aldo + Hannie van Eyck Foundation and Archive. She loves watching balls hovering in mid-air.

PAUL GANGLOFF
is a graphic designer who is interested in the practices of publishing and uses of notation that complicates the history of graphic design. The first time he saw a type ball was in the office of his grandfather's bookstore, in the early 1990s.

JULIA GEIGER
is an art historian and curator, and director of the Archiv Geiger in Munich. She appreciates bouncy balls and ball gowns in equal measure.

ELIOT HAWORTH
is a writer and assistant editor of Fantastic Man magazine. In his early teens he once did over 100 keepy uppies with a football, a fact that still makes him irrationally proud and overconfident in his actual footballing abilities.

ERNST VAN DER HOEVEN
is an Amsterdam-based collector of odd things, a gardener and a beekeeper. At a young age his love for symmetry was brutally disturbed when he lost one ball in a painful bike accident. In Dutch they call that a *bikkel*.

NICOLAI HOWALT
is a Danish artist whose photographic work spans documentary, conceptual and installation art. His relationship with the Ball is restricted to mundane ones: footballs, tennis balls and handballs.

GUUS KAANDORP
is a photographer and illustrator living and working in Amsterdam. He got accepted into art school with a series of pictures of friends throwing a bungalow home's furniture into a tree in order to get a football out of it.

LERNERT & SANDER
are artists and filmmakers that are known for their conceptual art films and eye-catching installations. In his youth, Sander used to be a fanatic tennis player in suburban Alkmaar. He never made it to the top because of his obsession with treating all tennis balls equally.

SUSAN MILLER
is a New York City based author and publisher of Astrologyzone.com. She loves ball gowns, meatballs, and avoids the terrifying whiffle ball.

MERIJN OUDENAMPSEN
studied political science and sociology. He used to play football. Now he reads and writes and cultivates his identity crisis.

VÉRONIQUE PATTEEUW
is an architect, researcher and editor based in Brussels. Her ongoing research focuses on the potential of unbuilt architecture, which explains her interest in the enigmatic spheres of the 19th century.

ANANDA PELLERIN
is a writer and editor with a focus on food, philosophy and culture. She has fond memories of watching her Italian-American grandmother making meatballs. She will never tell the secret ingredient.

ENZO PÉRÈS-LABOURDETTE
is an illustrator and author. He is proud to say his home is a safe ball-free zone, and will probably remain so.

SCHELTENS & ABBENES
are still life artists/photographers working and living in Amsterdam. Their relationship with the ball is one of hiding, covering their heads with hands and arms to cushion the impact.

LINDSAY SEKULOWICZ
is an artist and writer. The best ball she ever met was a giant pill millipede she found in a Malaysian forest while on an entomological expedition, which lived with her on a diet of sandalwood and rotting leaves.

JACK SELF
is an architect and editor-in-chief of *Real Review*. He thinks the meaning of life is to have a ball.

ADANIA SHIBLI
is a writer and cultural researcher. Since she was very young, she's been hoping to get a proper ball with no holes in it.

LILIAN STOLK
is an emoji expert, programmer on visual culture, digital illustrator, and a lover of the disco ball in the middle of her apartment, which turns the living room into a ballroom when the sun shines bright.

WOLFGANG TILLMANS
is an artist based in Berlin and London. Fascinated by astronomy from a very young age, Tillmans is ever inspired and moved by the wonder and mechanics of the solar system.

MARIETTE WIJNE
lives and writes in Amsterdam. For years she suffered from whiplash. At least that's what she thought. Until she exchanged the great green yoga ball for a decent office chair. After two days her mysterious back pain was gone.

MACGUFFIN
Biannual Magazine
Issue N° 6 The Ball
Autumn/Winter 2018

Cover: Wolfgang Tillmans, *Venus Transit, Edge* and *Venus Transit*, 2004

EDITORS-IN-CHIEF
Kirsten Algera
Ernst van der Hoeven

INTERNS
Verena Hahn, Marius Steiger

GRAPHIC DESIGN
Sandra Kassenaar

GRAPHIC DESIGN ASSISTANCE
Line-Gry Hørup

FINAL EDITOR
Billy Nolan

TRANSLATIONS
Robin Moger, Mike Ritchie, Liz Waters

CONTRIBUTORS
Kirsten Algera, Ivan Bennewith, Christine Bjerke, Merel Boers, Pol Esteve, Rosie Eveleigh, Fahri, Paul Gangloff, Julia Geiger, Eliot Haworth, Nicolai Howalt, Guus Kaandorp, Mathijs Labadie, Lernert & Sander, Susan Miller, Véronique Patteeuw, Ananda Pellerin, Enzo Pérès-Labourdette, Merijn Oudenampsen, Scheltens & Abbenes, Lindsay Sekulowicz, Jack Self, Adania Shibli, Lilian Stolk, Wolfgang Tillmans, Tessa van Eyck Wickham, Ernst van der Hoeven, Mariette Wijne

THANK YOU
Marijke Annema, Jan Boelen, Marie-Hélène Cornips, Peter-Frank Heuseveldt, Bart Gorter, Rudy Guedj, Perry De Jong, Gert Jonkers, Chris Kabel, Armin Lorenz, Petra Noordkamp, Martin Samson, Lou van Staaveren, Adam Štěch, Franziska Straubinger, Suzanne Veenman, Lieke Zuiderwijk and to our football team: Rudy, Marius, Xu, Mathias, Lou, Alexis, Thibault, Waèl, Zip, Daan and Suzy.

DISTRIBUTION
Export Press
36, rue des Petits Champs
75002 Paris, France
www.exportpress.com

Antenne Books
17, Amhurst Terrace
London E82BT, United Kingdom
www.antennebooks.com

Idea Books
Nieuwe Herengracht 11
1011 RK Amsterdam, The Netherlands
www.ideabooks.nl

If you would like to know more about distributing MacGuffin Magazine in your store or can't find it in your country please write to:
mail@macguffinmagazine.com

SUBSCRIPTIONS
Bruil & Van de Staaij
Douwenmaat 6
Meppel, The Netherlands
info@bruil.info

ADVERTISING
For advertising, media partnerships and special project opportunities:
ads@macguffinmagazine.com

PRINTING AND LITHOGRAPHY
NPN Drukkers, Breda
The Netherlands

MacGuffin is printed on Fedrigoni's Arcoprint Milk 1.5, 85 g/m², Fedrigoni's Freelife Vellum, 170 g/m² and Igepa's Magno Star, 115 g/m², typeset in Gothic 725 BT and Churchward Newstype.

MACGUFFIN OFFICES
Singel 76
1015 AC Amsterdam
The Netherlands
mail@macguffinmagazine.com
www.macguffinmagazine.com

SPECIAL THANKS TO
Ace & Tate, Amsterdam
Archiv Geiger, Munich
Bumper Experience, Amsterdam (bumperexperience.nl)
Bernie Bernthaler, Berlin (soundcloud.com/bernie-bernthaler)
François Dallegret, Montréal
ECAL, Lausanne
Fedrigoni, Brussels
FC RKVV Dia, Teteringen
MagCulture, London
Stack, London

MACGUFFIN PUBLISHING
© 2018 Reproduction without permission prohibited

ISSN 2405-8203

DISCLAIMER
MacGuffin Magazine has been careful to contact all copyright holders of the images used. If you claim ownership of any of the images presented here, and have not been properly identified, please contact MacGuffin and we will be happy to make a formal acknowledgement in a future issue.

MacGuffin is kindly supported by:

FONDS 21   FEDRIGONI

creative industries fund NL   Design/Miami/Basel

Inside back cover:
Artist Alighiero Boetti always preferred collaborative initiatives over individual efforts. In the 1970s, he recruited multiple teams of art students in Rome to execute *The Biro Drawings*, large sheets of paper covered with densely hatched fields of ballpoint pen ink. The title of this work, *Mettere al mondo il mondo*, 1975 (160 × 347 cm), expresses one of Boetti's working principles, suggesting that artists should not invent but rather bring preexisting material into their work in order to call renewed attention to their surroundings. © Tornabuoni Art